The Best of the Family Cookbook Project Cookbook

Favorite recipes from families across America

ISBN 978-0-9820243-0-0

Published by Family Cookbook Project, LLC
PO Box 262 W Simsbury CT 06092 (printed in Canada)
Family Cookbook Project - Helping families collect
cherished recipes forever. Visit us on the Web at
www.familycookbookproject.com

Welcome to the Best of the Family Cookbook Project Cookbook!

These fantastic recipes were hand selected by the editors of more than 150 family cookbooks as their best. Some are simple everyday favorites and some are the prized "family get-together" show stoppers. All of them are beloved by the families that submitted them.

Every family has treasured recipes, beloved as much for the memories they evoke, as it is for the taste. Often those recipes have been handed down orally through generations, or squirreled away on index cards or scraps of paper. A family cookbook is a way to gather, organize and share this wealth of family culinary favorites.

The Family Cookbook Project was started in 2004 when Bill Rice wanted to start a family cookbook and enlisted his high school friend Chip Lowell to help build a website to make the process easier. Before long, we found that other people had started using our website and loved it. We added additional tools, a nice design and began to promote it.

Five years later, we have helped more than 10,600 families and fundraising organizations gather and organize personal cookbooks. More than 40,000 individuals have contributed more than 232,000 recipes to the Family Cookbook Project and the best of those recipes are here for you to enjoy.

We both would like to thank our wives, Michelle Rice and Sally Lowell who inspire us to try new things both in life and at the dinner table. We also extend a special thanks to Ginny Larkin for editing and proofreading talents. Also we need to recognize our mothers, siblings, aunts and uncles, cousins and our kids who make up our extended families. They provide the good times and treasured memories that make having a family gathering worthwhile.

Bill Rice and Chip Lowell

P.S. If you like what you see here, you can start your own cookbook. It's easy, fun and affordable to create a lasting treasure of culinary memories. Learn how at FamilyCookbookProject.com.

Thank you to the Editors...

Each recipe lists the name of the contributor and the family cookbook, but here we recognize those individuals who are responsible for leading the creation of their family's cookbook and making the best of those recipes available to you in this best of Cookbook.

Take note of the photography on the section dividers. Each photo used was submitted by the editor themselves. We used exactly what was sent, which we feel gives this cookbook a special "feel."

Annette Ahart *2008 Ahart Family Reunion Cookbook*
Nancy Alvord *Family Recipes To Remember*
Keri Anderson *The Anderson / Farinella Family Cookbook*
Karen Atwell *Four Generations of Johnson Women*
Jeannine Ball *Cookin' with Balls -- Again!*
Marie Bateman *'We Love You Alison' Cookbook*
Mary Ann Behm *Grandma Bennett's recipes*
Maribeth Bennett *Bennett's & Beyond: A Family Cookbook*
Mary Blakeman *McCarthy Family Cookbook*
Reneé Bowers Bundy *Cooking With The Cousins*
Cheryl Brown *McKee Cooks*
Renee Bundy *Home Sweet Home Recipes*
Rhonda Calabro *The Calabro Family Cookbook Project*
Melinda Carreon *My Grandma's Kitchen*
Kelly Champlin Church *The Lucky Duck Cookbook*
Karen Christiansen *The Kearney Family Cookbook*
Annie Laurie Cisneros *Joy of the Repast: Favorite Recipes of Family and Friends*
Gloria Cody *All My Children Gotta Eat*
Carolyn Collins *Southern Family Cookbook Project*
Mary Jo Creevy *Mary Jo's Family Cookbook Project*
Shelley Cummins *The Wedding Cookbook for Jenna and Adam*
Connie Davis *The Hixon Family and Friends Cookbook Project*
DeeDee Duffy *The DiSalvatore Family Cookbook*
Harriet Duhe' Melancon *A Taste of Our Family*
Gerry Durkin *The Rogers' Girls Family Cookbook*
June Edwards *The Edwards - Buck Family and Friends Cookbook*
pamela ekman *Our family and friends cookbook project*
Stacey Empson *The Wiersch Family Cookbook*
Lee English *The English Family Recipe Treasury*
Theresa Erickson *The LaGuire/Putney Family Cookbook Project*
Diane Erickson *The Zuelke Family Cookbook*
Dorene Fankhauser *The Snyder/Johnson Family Cookbook Project*
Heather Fong *The Shogren Family Cookbook*
Vicki and Neil Frederiksen *Roebken Family Cookbook*
Donnalee Geiger *Our Family Favorites Cookbook*
Tanya Goodman *Goodman Family and Friends Cookbook Favorites*

Robin Gordon *The Gordon/Schorr Family Cookbook*
Paulette Hackman *Our Great Family*
Beverly Hanson *Hanson Family Cookbook*
Sharon Heath *The Whitcher Family Descendants Cookbook*
Julie Hodge *The Chappell Hodge Family Cookbook*
JoAn Howerton *The Brown Robbins Cookbook*
Kim Isaac *Eating with the Wolf Family*
Cathy Janet *Cathy's Favorites*
Isabelle Johnson *5 o:clock...Suppers Ready!*
Judie Jones *Buzzard's Best*
Alexandra Kantar *The Great Family Cookbook Project*
Jackie King *Memories*
Lee Kleinman *The Kleinman Family Cookbook*
Marilee Larkey *Mom Loves to Cook*
Shanna Lasley *The Lasley's Favorite Cookbook*
Wendy Lotze *Favorite Recipes*
Sally Lowell *The Robert S. Fouts Family and Friends Cookbook*
Susan Lyon *Mama's Little Black Book and More*
karen Malone *Recipes from Nannie Karen's Kitchen*
Erika Manning *The Friends and Family Cookbook Project*
Joyce Manwiller *Joyce Manwiller's Recipe Box*
Melissa Martin *The Martin Family Cookbook*
Frank Mattera *Francesco Mattera and Family Recipes*
Janet May *Fiesta!*
Beth Medlin *Our Family Recipes*
Harriet Melancon *The Tasty Bourgeois Cookbook*
Brenda Neroni *A Fine Collection of Yum*
Rick Newman *Cooking Across The Generations: The Newman/ Poulin Family Cookbook*
Elizabeth Newmeyer *Herring Heritage Cookbook*
Milly Noah *Grits to Gourmet*
Nita Orndorff *Grammy's Family Cookbook: A Selection of Our Family's Favorite Recipes*
Doris Parkins *Parkins Family Cookbook*
Sandra Perales *McMillan Family and Friends Cookbook*
Lorraine Plantz *The Toledo Area Chapter APA Celebrates National Payroll Week!*
Susan Privot *Family Recipes*
sabreena rabun *The Wellness Cookbook*
Fran Rajotte *Italian-American Cuisine*
Karen Rankin *The Rankin Family Cookbook Project*
Nancy Register *Family Favorites*
William Rice *The New Donovan Family Cookbook Volume II*
Sheila Rich *The Baptist Heritage Cookbook*
Ann Richardson *The Richardson Family Cookbook*
Marilyn Rome *The Rome Family Cookbook Project*
Cindy Rosarbo *La Famiglia Campano*
Tona Sauvageau *The Sauvageau Family Cookbook 2009*
Kathy Schew *Trickey Pond Family Reunion Cookbook*

Linda Schleker *The Schuldt Family Cookbook*
Brenda Seals *A Double Portion*
Jackie Shields *The Jones-Simpson Cookbook*
June Sloan *The Jeansonne Family Cookbook Project*
Dawn-Marie Sneed *Dawn-Marie's Favorite Family and Cookbook Recipes*
Maleah Snipes *The Snipes Family Cookbook Project*
Pat Spears *Mom's Favorite Recipes*
Anne Stokes *A. T. Cooks "Afternoon Tea" and other family recipes*
Kimberly Story *The Cookbook of Our Favorite Foods and Memories*
Susan Stroink Pickering *Oma Stroinks Recipes*
Robyn Stuart *The Hebert Family Cookbook Project*
Jean Thayer *Memories of Love, Cooking and Great Smells!*
Sherry Thompson *Mom's Recipe Box*
Marthalou Thompson *The Thompson Family Cookbook*
Patricia Thrasher-Waller *The Thrasher Family Cookbook Project*
Lynda Tolar *Cookbook Worthy*
Joyce Van Sessen *The Van Sessen Family Cookbook Project*
Janice Vold *The Vold Family Cookbook Project*
Lauren Vreeland-Long *The Vreeland Family Cookbook Project*
Wil Wagner *Aelred and Rita Wagner Family Cookbook*
Mike Wallace *A Real Southern Comfort*
Edie Ward *Edie's Family Cookbook*
Michiele Ward *The Ward/Bagley/Blevins and Friends Family Cookbook*
Edith Warner *The Warner Family and Friends' Cookbook*
Terry Wasson *Our Family Cookbook*
Terry Wasson *The Wasson Family Cookbook*
Sarah Watson *The McCullough Family Cookbook*
Melissa Wester *Morley Girls' Recipes & More!*
cheryl wright *Cooking with Family and Friends*
Lamar Yarbrough *Our Family Cookbook*
Aimee Zappa *Food for Friends*

Start Your Own Family Cookbook Today!

You too can begin the truly rewarding experience of creating a treasured heirloom – a personalized family cookbook.

Family cookbooks are an important way to preserve our mealtime traditions for future generations. With the passing of our loved ones comes the loss of treasured food traditions. Once the recipes are preserved online, they can be shared with other family members by email, individual printed recipes or in your own professionally printed cookbook.

Getting started is easy and fun.

1) Set up your Family Cookbook Project account at www.FamilyCookbookProject.com. All we need is some basic information and you can start entering your beloved recipes.

2) Use our email invitation tool to invite your family members to contribute their favorite recipes.

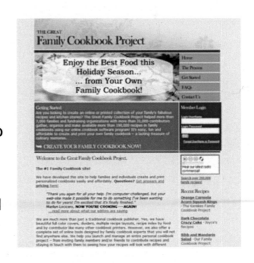

3) Select a cover, dividers and page layouts available from us or create your own. Edit your recipes, write an introduction and place your order. Our printer will deliver your family's personalized cookbooks in just 2-3 weeks!

It's that simple!

We would like to thank the many Family Cookbook Project editors that have helped us create this fabulous cookbook. Their dedication and commitment to preserving their own family food collections and their willingness to share the best of the best has made this cookbook possible.

Join the more than 40,000 family cookbook contributors who have used FamilyCookbookProject.com to make their family cookbook. We have created online tools to make the collection, organization, design and printing of your cookbook almost effortless – without having to be a computer expert!

Who knows, maybe your recipes will be included in the next edition of "Best of Family Cookbook Project"!

Table of Contents

Appetizers & Beverages

Allie's Football Dip pg. 15

Bacon Cheese Dip with Round Bread pg. 16

Cheese Puffs pg. 19

Aaron's Cocktail Franks

Aaron Heizer from Bennett's & Beyond: A Family Cookbook

1 56 oz package of cocktail franks
1 45 oz bottle of your favorite Barbeque sauce
1 small 8 oz jar of grape jelly

Pour all of the above ingredients into a crock pot, and let it cook on low (the longer the better) until ingredient flavors have combined.

Allie's Football Dip

Allie Bourgeois from The Tasty Bourgeois Cookbook

2 lbs lean ground beef
2 can rotel (medium) unless you like it hot!
2 blocks Mexican Velveeta
seasoning to taste (I use Tony's or Lemoins)

Brown the beef, drain off excess oil. Add the rotel and cheese, heat over medium/low heat until cheese is melted. Serve with Scoops!

Artichoke & Parmesan Dip

Susan Hoffman from The Wedding Cookbook for Jenna and Adam

1 can (8 oz.) water packed artichoke hearts (not marinated)
1 c. mayonnaise
1 c. parmesan cheese, grated
1/2 tsp. garlic salt
paprika to taste

Blend all indgredients in food processer or blender until artichokes are finely chopped. Bake in a covered casserole dish at 350º, for 20 minutes. Transfer to a hot dip bowl and sprinkle with paprika. Serve with warm sourdough or French bread.

Asparagus Wrapped with Prosciutto

Susan & Rich Landa, Vince's Family from 2008 Ahart Family Reunion Cookbook

2 pound fresh asparagus
8 slices prosciutto, thinly sliced
24 wontons
Butter, melted
Soy Sauce

Cut prosciutto into 24 pieces. Wash asparagus and break off tough ends - they will snap easily at the point where the stem becomes tender. Steam asparagus until it just becomes tender. Try not to over cook. Can be done ahead of time.

Preheat oven to 400 degrees.

Wrap asparagus with a slice of prosciutto, then wrap with a wonton. Brush with melted butter. Bake in oven until the wonton turns light brown. Place on serving dish and drizzle with soy sauce and serve.

Backpacker's Sweet Tea Mix

Wendy Lotze from Favorite Recipes

1 c. Nestea Sweetened Iced Tea Mix
2 c. Powdered Tang
1/2 c. Powdered Lemonade
1 c. Sugar
1/2 tsp. ground cloves

Mix all dry ingredients together in a resealable plastic bag. To make 1 serving, bring 1 cup of water to a boil. Add 1 tbsp. of mix to a mug and add water. Stir well. Can make cold tea, too. A refreshing, sweet treat on the trail.

Bacon Cheese Dip with Round Bread

Gina Bundy Noonan from Cooking With The Cousins

3/4 lb. bacon, cooked and crumbled
12 oz. sour cream
8 oz. softened cream cheese
2 c. shredded cheddar cheese
1 1/2 tsp. Worcestershire
1 lb. round sourdough bread

Beat cream cheese. Add sour cream, cheddar cheese and Worcestershire sauce. Add bacon. Mix. Cut out the center of the round bread, reserve for dipping. Put mixture in bread, wrap in foil and bake approximately 1 hour at 350°. The center of the bread does not go as far as the dip. Add extra crackers in order to enjoy all of the dip.

Baked Marinated Hot Wings

Dawn-Marie Sneed from Dawn-Marie's Favorite Family and Cookbook Recipes

4 lb. bag party chicken wings
1 1/2 bottles Louisiana Hot Sauce
4 pkg. Good Seasons Italian Dressing
1/2 c. lemon juice
1/2 stick butter, melted

Place wings into baking dish or bowl. Mix all other ingredients and pour over wings. Bake at 400° for an hour or until meat is falling from the bones.

Baked Pizza Dip

Marilyn Rome from The Rome Family Cookbook Project

1 8oz. cream cheese spread
1 tsp. Italian seasonings
1/8 tsp. garlic powder
1 pkg. Shredded Mozzarella cheese
1/2 c pizza sauce
2 tbsp. chopped green pepper
2 tbsp. chopped red pepper

Beat cream cheese and seasonings with electric mixer on medium speed until all ingredients are mixed. Spread on bottom of a 9" pie plate. Top with 1 cup of mozzarella cheese, pizza sauce and remaining 1 cup of mozzarella cheese and peppers. Bake at 350 degrees for 15-20 minutes or until mixture is thoroughly heated and cheese has melted. Serve with breadsticks or french bread.

Banana Punch

Karen Malone from Recipes from Nannie Karen's Kitchen

5 Ripe bananas (mashed)
1 2\3 cup water
1 cup sugar
1 frozen (can) orange juice
1 frozen (can) lemonade
1 large can pineapple juice
4 liters ginger ale
1 pkg. Kool aid (sweetened 6 cup pink or orange)

Mix together bananas, water, sugar and Kool-aid and then freeze. Take out 2 hours before drinking, then add frozen juices and ginger ale. I separate half the banana mixture and freeze separate and only use half mixture and half the pop at a time. Makes a lot of punch.

Basil, Cheese,Tomato and Pesto Appetizers

Nancy Alvord from Family Recipes To Remember

1 Pie Crust(freshly made or frozen)
3/4 cup Pesto Sauce
1 cup Sundried Tomatoes
1 cup Goat Cheese
3/4 cup toasted Pine Nuts

Roll pie crust thin into a 18 X 9 inch rectangular. Spread crust with pesto. Then put tomatoes over top the pesto followed by the goat cheese and then the pine nuts. Roll up from the long side. Seal the edge real good. Slice into 1 inch slices, Lay on a cookie sheet and cook until the pie crust is light golden brown.

Better Cheddar

William Rice from The New Donovan Family Cookbook Volume II

1 bar Cracker Barrel Vermont Cheddar
6-8 slices cook bacon crumbled
1 large bunch scallions chopped to 1/2 green stems
3/4 cup toasted walnuts
1/2 cup mayo

Grate cheese. Mix ingredients and serve on crackers or bread. Add additional mayo to desired consistancy if mixure is dry.

Ceviche

Maighan, Donovan and Dexter from Memories

3 lbs small raw shrimp, cleaned (Use other seafood such as Cod, Scallops, Clams, etc.)
4 Large tomatoes, seeded and diced
6 limes, juiced
4 lemons, juiced
1 cup cilantro leaves, chopped
1 Serrano Chile, seeded and finely chopped (we use jalapenos for more spice)
½ of a cucumber, peeled and diced
1 red onion, diced
Salt and pepper to taste
3 tablespoons tomato sauce (we use Clamato Juice sometimes)

Lay out shrimp (seafood) in the bottom of a glass baking dish. Pour lemon and lime juice over them and refrigerate for 3 hours. The juice will "cook" the shrimp. Toss remaining ingredients and refrigerate for one more hour or longer. Enjoy with tortilla chips or on top of grilled fish.

We use different seafood depending on what's fresh or on sale. Cod and Scallops are favored by most people. Maighan likes her Ceviche much thicker and I like mine with much more juice so we will sometimes add straight clam juice to thin out and add flavor. The more Jalapenos the better for me and seeds will add a lot of heat.

Cheese and Sausage Balls

Fran Rajotte from Italian-American Cuisine

1 lb. hot sausage
2 cups grated sharp Cheddar cheese
3 cups Bisquick or 2 1/2 cups Bisquick and 1/2 cup water

Mix all ingredients together. Roll into small round balls. Heat oven to 350 degrees. Bake for 20 minutes.

Cheese Appetizer

Kathleen & John Gereski from The Calabro Family Cookbook Project

3 TB Fresh Parsley
3 TB Fresh Basil
3 TB Scallions
3 Cloves Garlic
1 tsp Sugar
1/2 tsp salt
1/2 tsp pepper
1/2 c. White wine vinegar
4 oz. chopped pimento
2 Bricks Vermont Cheddar Cheese
2 - 8 oz. packages of cream cheese or 1 package of cheese alternative

Mix all marinade ingredients together (everything except the cheese) and pour over the sliced cheddar/cream cheeses (alternating pattern of cheese as you lay it out in a small serving dish) Refrigerate several hours or overnight.

Cheese Petit Fours

Beth Medlin from Our Family Recipes

1 lb margarine
4 jars Kraft Old English Cheese Spread
1-1/2 tsp Worcestershire sauce
1 tsp tabasco sauce
1 tsp onion powder
dash caynne pepper
3 loaves Pepperidge Farm thin slice sandwich bread

Use electric knife to remove crust from bread. Mix all other ingredients together. Using 3 slices of bread, spread filling between slices. Cut into 6 slices or pieces. (the electric knife works well) Sprinkle top of cut sandwiches with caynne pepper. Place sandwiches on cookie sheet and set in freezer until frozen. Place in ziplock bags until ready to bake. Bake frozen at 350° 15-20 min. Serve warm.

Personal Notes: These will keep in the freezer for several weeks.

Cheese Puffs

Terri McCarthy from McCarthy Family Cookbook

2 c. sharp cheddar cheese (grated)
1 c. flour
½ c. margarine (softened)
½ tsp. paprika
½ tsp. cayenne pepper
½ tsp. salt
50 small olives, stuffed

Blend cheese and softened margarine. Stir in flour and seasonings. Wrap 1 teaspoon mixture around each olive. covering completely. Shape into a small pyramid. Arrange on a cookie sheet and chill. These puffs can also be frozen before baking. Bake at 350° F for 20 minutes. Serve hot.

Chinese Crispy Spring Rolls

Rick & Amy Boyce from La Famiglia Campano

1 c. bean sprouts
1 bunch scallions
2 carrots (julienne cut)
2/3 c. bamboo shoots - (julienne)
1 1/2 c. white mushrooms sliced
3-4 Tbsp. vegetable oil
1 tsp. salt
1 tsp. light brown sugar
1 tsp. light soy sauce
1 T. Chinese rice wine or dry sherry
40 or so spring roll wrappers
1 T. cornstarch paste
oil for deep-frying

To make cornstarch paste: mix 4 parts dry cornstarch with about 5 parts cold water until smooth.

Heat oil in a wok and stir-fry the vegetables for about 1 min. Add salt, sugar, soy sauce and rice wine or sherry and stir fry for 1 1/2 - 2 minutes. Remove and drain the excess liquid, then let cool.

Appetizers & Beverages

To make spring rolls: cut each wrapper in half diagonally, then place about 1 T. of the vegetable mixture 1/3 way down the wrapper, with the triangle pointing away from you. Lift the lower flap over the filling and roll it up once. Fold both ends and roll it again. Brush a little cornstarch paste to finish rolling.

Heat oil until hot. Add 8-10 and deep fry for 2-3 minutes. Serve with duck sauce or soy sauce if desired.

Chipped Beef Cheese Ball

Doris Parkins from Parkins Family Cookbook

3 - 3 oz. pkgs. chipped beef, chopped fine
8 oz. pkg. cream cheese at room temperature
2 T. Worcestershire sauce
1/4 c. chopped onion
1 T. Accent

Mix two pkgs. beef and other ingredients. Mix well. Make 2-3 balls. Roll in third pkg. of chipped beef.

Coconut Shrimp with Pina Colada Dipping Sauce

Judie Jones from Buzzard's Best

Dip
½ cup sour cream
¼ cup Cream de Coco or Pina Colada Mix (no Alcohol)
¼ cup crushed canned pineapple
2 Tbl Coconut Rum
Pinch of coconut

Salsa
2 med Roma Tomatoes Diced
3 Tbl diced white onion
3 Tbl chopped Cilantro
2 tsp fine chopped Serrano or jalapeno pepper

Shrimp
6-8 cups canola (as required by your fryer)
12 large shrimp cleaned and deveined leave tails on
1 ½ cups tempura flour
¼ tsp salt
1 cup milk
1 cup Panko, Japanese bread crumbs
½ cup shredded coconut

Mix together and chill dip ingredients
Mix salsa ingredients in a bowl and chill while you make the shrimp.
Heat oil to 350 degrees
Mix tempura flour, milk and salt together let stand for 5 minutes.
Combine panko and shredded coconut.
Dip shrimp in wet mixture then dredge in dry mixture, pressing to adhere.
Hold shrimp by the tail and slowly lower into the hot oil 2-3 minutes until golden. Drain on paper towels.

Just before serving add the salsa to the dipping sauce and stir slightly, dip or spoon on shrimp.

Do ahead all but the frying, cover and refrigerate up to 8 hours. Keep some of the dry ingredients to re coat if they seem soggy.

Cranberry Salsa

Heather Hanson from Hanson Family Cookbook

12 oz. fresh cranberries rinsed
1 apple
4 fresh jalapenos without seeds for MILD
8 fresh jalapenos with seeds for HOT
6-8 green onions
2-3 big handfuls of cilantro leaves
3/4 to 1 c. sugar or Splenda (the more heat, the more sugar)

Add all to food processor and mix until well blended.

Serve with tortilla chips.

Crawfish-Artichoke Havarti Cheese Bisque

Norris Yarbrough from Our Family Cookbook

2 sticks of butter
1/2 cup diced onion
1/4 cup diced green bell pepper
1/4 cup diced celery
1 tablespoon garlic
1/2 cup flour
2 teaspoons salt
2 pints half & half
2 cups chicken broth
1/2 teaspoon thyme
2 teaspoons hot sauce
1/4 pound Havarti cheese
1 pound crawfish tails
1/4 cup minced parsley
1/4 cup minced green onions
2-14 ounce cans quartered artichoke hearts, drained

1. Heat butter in a heavy pan over low to medium heat. Add onion, bell pepper, celery and garlic; cook until onions start to turn clear.
2. Add flour and cook for additional 5 minutes being careful not to brown flour.
3. Whisk in half & half, then chicken stock until sauce is smooth and creamy. Add thyme, salt, artichoke hearts and hot sauce; simmer for 10 minutes stirring occasionally.
4. Add cheese and continue to cook until cheese is melted. Stir in crawfish tails and continue to simmer for 15 minutes until crawfish are heated thoroughly.
5. Stir in parsley and green onions.

Cucumber Sandwiches

Karen Rankin from The Rankin Family Cookbook Project

2 tsp dill seed
8 oz whipped cream cheese
 pkg dry Italian dressing mix
1 lb rye bread sliced
1 cucumber thinly sliced
1/2 cup mayo

Mix dill, cream cheese, mayo and dressing mix

Spread on rye bread slices
Top with cucumber slice

Fruit Slush Punch

Barbara Mothershead from Mom's Favorite Recipes

2 1/2 c. or 20oz pineapple juice
1 12oz can frozen orange juice
1 12oz can frozen lemonade
3 bananas, mashed
2 c. sugar
4 c. water
2 qt. lemon-lime beverage
2 qt. Seven-up

Mix thoroughly all the ingredients except the pop; freeze. When ready to serve, stir to a mush; add lemon-lime beverage and Seven-up.
Yield: 25 servings.

Glühwein (mulled wine)

Kathy Schew from Trickey Pond Family Reunion Cookbook

750 ml bottle of inexpensive dry red wine
2/3 cup of raw cane sugar or white sugar
Juice and peel of one small lemon
2 cardamom pods
4 cloves
2 bay leaves
2 cinnamon sticks

Put everything in a heavy bottomed pan. Stir to melt the sugar. Heat the mixture over low heat, and leave for about an hour - it should never boil, just sort of seethe.

Serve in small mugs (straining out the peel and spices), with optional shot of brandy, kirsch or other liqueur.

Personal Notes: Increase the amount proportionately to serve more people. Vary the sweetener to change the taste - honey is interesting, as is dark brown sugar or molasses.

Homemade Salsa

Bill and Jennifer Roebken from Roebken Family Cookbook

2 jalapeños
1/4 of an onion
1 tsp. pepper
1 Tbsp garlic salt
1 large can of whole tomatoes

Boil the jalapeños in water for 15 minutes. Cut off the top of the jalapenos. In a blender, pulse onion, jalapeños, garlic salt and pepper. Add can of tomatoes and pulse again.

Hot Crab Dip

Sally Lowell from The Rob Fouts Family and Friends Fundraiser Cookbook Project

1 8 oz. package cream cheese
1 Tbs. milk
2 tsp. Worcestershire sauce
1 can lump crab meat-6-7 oz.
2 Tbsp. green onion finely chopped
2 Tbsp. toasted slivered almonds

Combine cream cheese, milk and Worcestershire sauce until well mixed. Add drained crabmeat and green onions. Bake in a shallow greased pie plate at 350° for 15 minutes. Top with toasted almonds. Serve with crackers or small pumpernickel slices.

Jalapeno Bacon Wraps

Robyn Stuart from The Hebert Family Cookbook Project

25-30 Jalapenos
2 lbs bacon--strips cut into 3 pieces
2 packages of cream cheese
toothpicks
(optional) 1 lb of cooked shrimp or crawfish

Cut Jalapenos in half lengthwise and remove seeds. fill each jalapeno half with cream cheese and 1 shrimp or crawfish. Then wrap with 1/3 of a bacon slice, Use toothpick to keep it together. Place on baking dish or pan. Bake at 450 degrees for 30 to 40 minutes or till bacon is cooked.

Kahluah

Mary Kratochvil from Grandma Bennett's recipes

2 cup water
2 tsp. glycerin (drug store)
3 3/4 cup granulated sugar
4/5 quart of vodka
2 tsp. vanilla
6 tbls. instant coffee mixed with 1/2 cup water

Boil sugar and water 40 minutes. Add vanilla, instant coffee mixed with water, glycerin & vodka. Mix well. Cool and bottle. Allow 21 days before using.

Mexican Cheese Ball

Carol & Dan Nagy from Eating with the Wolf Family

2 pkg (8 oz) cream cheese
1 pkg taco seasoning
1/2 jar 8 oz jalapeños
1 C shredded cheese

Let cream cheese soften. Drain and chop jalapeños; scrap from chopper onto paper towel to soak up excess moisture.

In medium size bowl, mix cream cheese, seasoning, and jalapeños. Shape as desired and cover with shredded cheese. Serve with crackers.

Mini Ham Puffs

Nita Orndorff from Grammy's family Cookbook

2 1/2 oz pkg of deli slice ham
1 small onion - finely diced
1/2 c shredded Swiss cheese
1 egg - lightly beaten
1 1/2 tsp Dijon mustard
1/4 tsp black pepper
1 tube refrigerated crescent rolls

Preheat oven to 350º. Finely dice the ham and onion. Place in a bowl and stir in the egg, pepper and mustard. Stir well. Spray 2 mini muffin pans with Pam. Unroll the crescent rolls and press out seams to form into two rectangles. Cut each into 12 squares. Place each piece of dough into a muffin cup and press up the sides. Spoon about 1 tablespoon of ham mixture into each cup. Do not overfill. Bake for 15 minutes or until lightly browned.

Momma Edna's Spaghetti Pie

Edna Mattera from Francesco Mattera and Family Recipes

1 pound linguine #8,
6 large eggs,
1 pound bacon,
6 ounces of thinly sliced pepperoni, (can buy presliced),
Salt and pepper,
6 ounces of grated cheese

In a large pot boil enough water to cook linguine as per package directions.

Cut bacon into little pieces and fry till crisp, when done place onto paper towels and let drain, save a little fat and set aside. Take sliced pepperoni and cut into 1/4's, set aside. In a separate bowl beat 6 eggs and add a good amount of salt and pepper. Now add in grated cheese and mix well, set aside.

After spaghetti is cooked, drain and place back in pot, add bacon and mix, then pepperoni and mix. Pour in egg mixture, saved fat and mix very well.

In a 9" round 2 to 3 inch deep frying pan pour in complete mixture. Push down to level mixture. Cover and cook on medium to low heat. After about 8 minutes, remove cover and lift frying pan and give little push. If mixture moves easily, its time for the tricky part.

Take a large dish and cover frying pan and turnover. Then slide the pie back into frying pan cover and cook another 8 minutes. Remove cover. Take dish and cover frying pan. Turnover and serve warm and sliced like a pie.

Mussels, Nova Scotia style

Paulette Hackman from Our Great Family

1 1/2 c white wine
1-2 stalks celery, chopped
1 large shallot, chopped
1 small clove garlic, chopped
1 tsp sea or kosher salt
1 tsp fresh ground pepper
1/4 tsp ground hot pepper
olive oil for sautéing
3 lbs. fresh mussels

Wash mussels in a sink full of water and remove "beards." Toss out any open mussels. (first, tap shell of said mussel and if it slowly closes, it is still good to go). Set aside. In a large pot, heat some good olive oil and saute veggies until softened, not brown. Add white wine or stock and bring to a gentle boil. Add mussels all at once, lower heat to medium, cover. In about 2 minutes, shake pot while still covered, to redistribute mussels. Check again in about 2 minutes. The mussels should all be open. Place in a large bowl, pour chopped veggies and broth over them and serve hot.
Note: low sodium chicken stock or combination of both can be used in place of the wine.

Newfoundland Fish Cakes

Rick Newman from Cooking Across The Generations: The Newman/ Poulin Family Cookbook

1 lb salt cod
2 cups mashed potato
1 cup chopped onions
1/2 cup chopped celery
3 tbsp butter
1 tbsp black pepper
1 tsp oregano
1/2 tsp nutmeg
1/2 cup bread crumbs
vegetable oil for frying
all purpose flour
1/4 cup finely chopped salt pork fried into scruncions

Soak the salt cod overnight in a bowl of water in the refrigerator. Change water 2 or 3 times.

Make the mash potatoes, gently saute the onions and celery in the butter for about 5 minutes, add the pepper, oregano and nutmeg mixing all ingredients together.

Add the vegetable mixture to the mashed potatoes.

Bring 3 quarts of water to a boil, add the cod, return to boil then reduce heat to a simmer. Cook for for 10-12 minutes. Drain immediately. Add the fish to the potato mixture and stir to break up fish and mix all ingredients.

Add bread crumbs if needed for body and mix together. Refrigerate for one hour.

Mold mixture into small to medium patties and place on a baking sheet sprayed with cooking spray. Refrigerate for four hours.

Heat oil over medium heat, sprinkle patties with flour and add about 5 patties to a pan, cook until brown [about 5 minutes] then turn carefully and brown the other side. For breakfast, serve with eggs, toast and tea.

Party Punch

Melissa Martin from The Martin Family Cookbook

1 pkg strawberry kool-aid
1 pkg cherry kool aid
1 lg can frozen orange juice
1 lg can frozen lemonade
1 qt ginger ale
2 C sugar
4 qts water or use some water and ice cubes

Combine all ingredients.

Portabella Mushroom Stuffed with Crab

Gianna Milletary from McKee Cooks

16 oz. can lump crab meat
1/2 c. mayonnaise
1 t. dry mustard
1/2 c. bread crumbs
1 pkg. McCormick Old Bay Crab Seasoning
8 med. Portabella mushrooms, stems and gills removed
1/2 c. grated Parmesan

Combine first 5 ingredients; mix gently to keep crab from breaking. Stuff mushroom caps with generous portion of crab; place on greased baking tray. Bake 20 minutes at 350°. Sprinkle with Parmesan or melt on mushrooms for last 5 minutes in oven.

Resbaladera from Costa Rica

Janet May from Fiesta!

1/2 lb. uncooked rice
4 cloves
2 sticks of cinnamon
1 pinch of nutmeg
1 c. milk
2 tsp. cornstarch
Sugar to taste

Soak the rice for two hours in a large pot. Add cloves, cinnamon, nutmeg and 3 c. of milk. Cook until the rice is very soft. Stir the cornstarch into the remaining milk and add to the pot. Cook until the mixture thickens slightly. Blend until smooth. Sweeten to taste. Chill well and serve.

Personal Notes: Note: if desired rice can be replaced with or half rice/half barley.

Salmon Mousse

Victoria Stroink from Oma Stroinks Recipes

½ cup heavy cream
1 Tbs. or 1 envelope unflavored gelatin
¼ cup cold water
½ cup boiling water
½ cup mayonnaise
1 Tbs. Fresh lemon juice
1 Tbs. Plus 1 tsp grated onion
½ tsp. Tabasco or hot sauce
1 tsp salt
2 Tbs. Finely chopped capers
½ tsp paprika
2 cups fresh salmon (poached, chilled, boned, and finely ground)

Whip heavy cream stiff but not dry.

1. Sprinkle the gelatin over the cold water in a bowl. Let stand to soften 5 minutes. Pour over this the boiling water- mix well with a wire wisk. Let cool to room temperature.

2. Add the mayonnaise, lemon juice, paprika, Tabasco, onion and salt – mix well. Add the caper and salmon – mix well.

3. Fold in the whipped cream and pour mixture into the fish mold. With a glass mold no oiling is necessary. Place mold in refrigerator for several hours until set.

4. To unmold, loosen the edge of the mousse from the mold with the tip of a knife. Place in the freezer section of a refrigerator or in a bowl of ice water for 15 minutes. The additional cold causes the mousse to harden and makes it easier to release. Turn the mold upside down and shake it or tap the edge lightly on a wooden or cushioned surface. When any part of the mousse begins to release, place it over the serving plate, as it is difficult to move once out of the mold. Garnish with lemon wedges and parsley.

See Salmon Mousse Dill Sauce recipe for topping.

Personal Notes: Canned Salmon well drained, may be substituted for fresh, although the flavor will not be as delicate nor as good.

Salmon Mousse Dill Sauce

Victoria Stroink from Oma Stroinks Recipes

1tsp salt
1/4 tsp white pepper
¼ cup fresh lemon juice
2 cups sour cream
3 tbs. finely chopped Dill

Combine ingredients, stir well, and refrigerate for several hours before using to let flavor develop.

If the Salmon Mousse is to be used as a luncheon entrée, this recipe will serve six to eight persons. The dill sauce should be served in a sauce boat or small pitcher to be poured over the mousse after it has been served.

As a first course for a more elaborate meal, This mousse will serve from eight to twelve persons. The Dill sauce should be served as above.

If the mousse is to be used as an hors d'oeuvre, the ¼ cup of lemon juice in the Dill Sauce should be replaced with the grated rind of one lemon (about one teaspoon full) and all liquid drained off the sour cream before mixing. This makes a slightly thicker sauce that can be used to outline the fish shape. A bed of lettuce leaves cupped toward the mousse will help to hold the sauce in place. This arrangement is very attractive on the hors d'oeuvre table and permits the guest to place some mousse and sauce on a cracker with no utensil other than a serving knife. When used in this manner, this recipe will yield from 100 to 150 servings.

Sausage, Sweet and Hot

Cathy Barbier Janet from Cathy's Favorites

1 lb hot smoked sausage, sliced, cooked and drained
1 cup brown sugar
2/3 cup ketchup
1/2 cup white vinegar
1/2 cup onion, chopped
2 tbsp Lea & Perrin sauce
10 drops Tabasco
1 tsp dry mustard
1 tsp salt
1/2 tsp pepper
3/4 cup Chili Sauce

Mix cooked sausage with all ingredients. Simmer 45 minutes and you have a great party dish!

Seven Layer Dip

Sara Schleker from The Schuldt Family Cookbook

1 (16 oz.) can refried beans
1 tsp. cumin
1 tsp. garlic powder
2 large avocados, mashed
1 tbsp. grated onion
1 c. sour cream
1 large tomato, chopped
1 c. chopped green onion
1 c. shredded cheddar cheese
1 c. shredded Monterey jack
1 c. sliced black olives

Mix refried beans, cumin, and garlic powder together. Layer on bottom of 8 by 8 inch pan. Mix avocado and grated onion and layer on top of refried beans. Layer on top of avocado in the following order: sour cream, cheddar cheese, Monterey jack cheese, tomato, green onion, and olive. Serve with taco chips.

Spinach Balls

Donnalee (Cater) Geiger from Our Family Favorites Cookbook

2 pkgs frozen chopped spinach, drained
2 c Pepperidge Farm herb dressing
4 eggs
1 lg onion
1 1/2 sticks butter
1/2 c Parmesan cheese
1/2 tsp garlic salt
1/2 tsp each of pepper, thyme, & accent (or other seasoning if you wish)

Cook and drain spinach thoroughly. Mix all ingredients and roll into quarter size balls and place on cookie sheet.

May freeze ahead if you wish. Bake 350* for 20 minutes

Stuffed Jalapeno's

Theresa Erickson from The LaGuire/Putney Family Cookbook Project

15 to 20 jalapenos
1 roll of Bob Evans Hot and Spicy Sausage
1 small package softened cream cheese
1/2 cup of shredded parmesan cheese
1/2 cup sour cream
dash of salt, pepper and garlic salt to taste

Cut jalapenos in half lengthwise, remove all seeds and scrape out all the white parts so they are not hot(be sure to wear protection on hands)

Fry up sausage, drain. Mix in all other ingredients. Stuff each pepper and lay in a 9 X 13 pan. Bake at 350 for 35-45 minutes, then put under broiler until they are brown on top.

Swedish Pickled Shrimp

June Edwards from The Edwards - Buck Family and Friends Cookbook

2 to 21/2 lbs. fresh or frozen shrimp
1/2 c. celery tops
1/4 c. mixed pickling spices
1 tbsp. salt
2 c. sliced onions
7-8 bay leaves
11/2 c. salad oil
3/4 c. white vinegar
3 tbsp. capers with juice
21/2 tsp. celery seed
11/2 tsp. salt
drops of bottled hot pepper sauce to taste

Cover shrimp with boiling water; add celery tops, pickling spices, and salt. Cover and simmer 5 minutes. Drain; peel and devein under cold water. (I sometimes use frozen shrimp that are all shelled and deveined.)
Layer shrimp, onion and bay leaves in a shallow casserole. Combine remaining ingredients. Pour over shrimp. Cover; chill at least 24 hrs. spooning marinade over shrimp occasionally.

Sweet & Sour Meatballs

Joan Downey from The Rogers' Girls Family Cookbook

1 lb Ground Beef
1/2 c Bread Crumbs
1/3 c Chopped Onions
1/4 c Milk
1 Egg
1 tsp Parsley
1 tsp Salt
1/2 tsp Pepper
1/2 tsp Worchestershire Sauce
12 oz bottle of chili sauce
8 oz jar of grape jelly

Mix together & form into small balls. Place on cookie sheet. Bake at 400 degrees for 12 to 15 minutes or until done. Take meatballs out & drain off grease. Heat chili sauce and grape jelly (any brand). Heat until jelly melts. Then add meatballs & simmer 30 minutes.

Taco Dip

Barbara Heafy from The Warner Family and Friends' Cookbook

1 can refried beans
1/2 - 3/4 packet of taco seasoning
1 pint sour cream
2-3 tomatoes diced and drained
1 small can of sliced black olives
1 sm. jar Jalapeno peppers, diced
2 cup package of finely shredded cheese

Cut sliced black olives into slightly smaller pieces (the can of chopped olives is not good).
Mix refried beans and taco seasoning in a small bowl.
Spread this mixture onto the bottom of a glass 9x13 pan.
Spread at least 3/4 to all of the sour cream over the beans.
The next layer is to sprinkle on the tomatoes (I try not to do this too far in advance of serving because the tomatoes can become too juicy)
Layer on the cheese, then olives and jalapeno peppers. (about 1/4 cup jalapeno peppers - it depends on how spicy you like it.)
Keep covered and chilled until serving.
Need tortilla chips for dipping.

Texas Toothpicks

Patricia Thrasher-Waller from The Thrasher Family Cookbook Project

large Jalapeño Peppers
cream cheese or block cheddar cheese
thin bacon slices

Rinse jalapeños, using food handler gloves, cut pepper in half, lengthwise. Remove the seeds. Fill halved peppers with choice of cheese, then wrap bacon slice around the pepper, secure bacon with a toothpick. Grill, turning often until bacon is crispy.

Vold's Killer Margaritas

Janice Vold from The Vold Family Cookbook Project

1 c. Jose Cuervo Tequila
1/3 c. Triple Sec (any brand)
1/6 c. Grand Marnier
3 c. Jose Cuervo margarita mix
Lime wedges

Mix first four ingredients together and pour over ice in glass. Squeeze wedge of lime in glass and toss in. Stir.

Warm Crab Dip

Melissa Connor from The Cookbook of Our Favorite Foods and Memories

1/2 C Milk
1/3 C Salsa
24 oz Cream Cheese
16 oz Imitation Crab Meat, flaked
1 C thinly sliced Green Onions

Soften cream cheese for 30 sec to 1 min in microwave to soften and make mixing easier. Mix all ingredients together. Transfer to a greased slow cooker, 1.5 quart works well. Heat on low for 2-3 hours, stirring often. Serve with crackers or rye bread.

West Indies Salad

Milly Noah from Grits to Gourmet

1 lb. lump crab meat - jumbo
1 medium onion - chopped
4 oz. Oil (Wesson)
3 oz. Apple cider vinegar
4 oz. Ice water
3 T of small capers (optional)

In a 2 quart dish layer 1/2 onion, 1/2 crab meat, then repeat layer. Sprinkle capers on top. Sprinkle with salt and pepper to taste. Pour ingredients in the following order; Oil, Vinegar then Water. Let marinate in refrigerator for at least 4 hours. Toss and serve with crackers.

Whitcher's Garage Radiator Flush Punch

Karon Davenport Nason 1954 from The Whitcher Family Descendants Cookbook

2 Cups Prepared Tea
Juice of 2 Oranges
1 - 12 ounce can of Orange Soda
Juice of 1 Lemon
1 Cup of Ginger Ale
Orange and Lemon Slices

In a pitcher combine all of the ingredients. Serve over ice.

White Pizza

Susan Privot from Family Recipes

4 tbsp olive oil
1 tbsp dry basil
4 cloves garlic, minced
¾ tsp red pepper flakes
2 c warm water
¼ c olive oil
2 tsp instant yeast
2 tsp salt
1 tbsp sugar
4-5 c bread flour
Fontina Cheese and Mozzarella Cheese, grated

Appetizers & Beverages

Simmer olive oil, basil, garlic and red pepper on very low heat till garlic softens and flavors blend. (I usually do this ahead and let it sit – it helps the flavor infuse into the oil).

With the regular beater bar, combine 2 c flour, salt, sugar, and instant yeast into mixing bowl. Mix till combined.

Add warm water and oil and mix until incorporated. Allow to rest 5-10 minutes.

Change to dough hook and continue mixing in flour until a nice firm dough forms (this should be about 2-3 more cups). It will pull aside from the bowl and 'knead' itself on the hook when there's enough flour. Transfer to a bowl sprayed with PAM, cover and let rise until doubled (2 hrs).

Punch down dough and form into 2 balls; let rest a few minutes.

Roll dough out (you may need to let it rest a few minutes if it keeps 'shrinking' up) onto counter sprayed with PAM. Either put it onto a pizza pan or a cookie sheet lined with parchment paper.

Top with olive oil mixture, and grated Italian cheeses.
Bake in a 500 degree preheated oven on the bottom rack until golden brown.

Worthington's Wonderful Winter Dip

Mama from Mama's Little Black Book and More

1 large eggplant
1 small onion, minced
2 tomatoes
3 tbsp. vinegar
2 slices bread, trimmed
1-1/2 tsp. salt
1/2 tsp. pepper
2 tbsp. sugar
4 tbsp. olive oil

Preheat oven to 350º.
Wash eggplant and place on cookie sheet. Bake whole for 1 hour (prick with a fork so it doesn't explode). Cool 30 minutes. Do not peel.

Soak bread in vinegar for a few minutes.

Dice eggplant into 1/2 to 1-inch squares. Add minced onions, chopped unpeeled tomatoes, bread soaked in vinegar, and remainder of ingredients.

Chill at least one hour.

Bread and Muffins

Sour Milk Doughnuts pg. 44

La Jolla French Toast pg. 43

6-Week Raisin Bran Muffins

JoAnne Anderson from Memories

1 (15oz.) box Raisin Bran cereal
3 c. sugar
5 c. flour
5 tsp. baking soda
2 tsp. salt
4 beaten eggs
1 c. oil
1 qt. buttermilk

Mix cereal, sugar, flour, salt and soda in a large bowl. Add beaten eggs, oil, and buttermilk mixing well. Store in a covered container (Tupperware) in refrigerator until desired. Will last up to 6 weeks in refrigerator; use as needed. Fill muffin cups 2/3 full and bake at 350º for 30 minutes.

Aunt Dovie's Old Fashioned Tea Cakes

Ellen Yarbrough from Our Family Cookbook

5 cups Self Rising Flour
2 cups Sugar
1 teaspoon baking soda
2 teaspoons baking powder
½ cup shortening
2 eggs
½ cup buttermilk
1 teaspoon vanilla

Preheat Oven to 375 degrees. Spray cookie sheet with non-stick spray. In a large bowl, sift flour, sugar, baking soda and baking powder. Cut in shortening with pastry knife or whisk. Add eggs, buttermilk and vanilla and mix until well blended. Knead until mixture is smooth. Pour mixture onto a lightly floured surface. (Use cutting board or parchment paper will do). Roll dough mixture approximately 1/4 - inch thick. Cut with cookie cutter (3 1/2 inch round). Place cookies 1 inch apart on lightly greased cookie sheet and bake at 375 degrees in oven on middle rack for 10 to 15 minutes (or until slightly brown). Remove from oven and place on wire rack to cool.

Baked Panettone Bread French Toast

Brenda Seals from A Double Portion

1/2 loaf of Panettone bread
5 eggs
½ cup coconut milk or half and half
1 tsp vanilla
1 tsp freshly grated nutmeg plus additional for topping

1. Slice Panettone Bread into 8-1 inch slices.
2. Mix eggs, coconut milk, vanilla and nutmeg.
3. Dredge slices into egg mix.
4. Place in Shallow dish and pour egg mixture over bread.
5. Cover and refrigerate 4 hours or overnight.
6. Grate fresh nutmeg over bread and bake in a preheated 350 degree oven for 25-30 minutes.

Banana Bread

Aunt Martha Wolf Ginn from Eating with the Wolf Family

1/2 cup butter
1 cup sugar
2 eggs
2 cups flour (unsifted)
1 tsp baking soda
3 T sour milk
1 cup chopped pecans
3 ripe bananas - mashed (very ripe bananas make the bread more moist)

To get small amount of sour milk, add 1 1/2 tsp lemon juice or vinegar to 1/4 cup sweet milk at room temperature. Let stand a few minutes. Measure out 3 T called for in recipe. Cream butter and sugar, blend in eggs. Sift together flour and baking soda and add to creamed mixture with sour milk. Blend in mashed banana. Turn into greased loaf pan; bake at 350 degrees about 1 hour or until center of loaf tests done.

Banana Chocolate Chip Muffins

Mary Jo Creevy from Mary Jo's Family Cookbook Project

2-3 extra ripe bananas
2 eggs
1 c. brown sugar
1/2 c. melted butter
1 t. vanilla
2-1/4 c. flour
2 t. baking powder
1/2 t. cinnamon
1/2 t. salt
1 c. chocolate chips
1/2 c. chopped walnuts

Slice bananas into blender and puree. Beat bananas, eggs, sugar, butter and vanilla until blended. Combine other ingredients and stir in chips and nuts. Add banana mixture. Mix until blended. Bake 350 25-30 minutes. Makes 12-18 muffins. They are DELICIOUS!!

Banana Sour Cream Bread

Doris Parkins from Parkins Family Cookbook

1/4 c. white sugar
1 tsp. ground cinnamon
3/4 c. butter
3 cups white sugar
3 eggs
6 very ripe bananas, mashed
1 (16 oz.) container sour cream
2 tsp. vanilla extract
2 tsp. ground cinnamon
1/2 tsp. salt
3 tsp. baking soda
4 1/2 cups all-purpose flour
1 c. chopped walnuts (optional)

Preheat oven to 300°. Grease four 7x3 inch loaf pans. In a small bowl, stir together 1/4 c. white sugar & 1 tsp. cinnamon. Dust pans lightly with cinnamon & sugar mixture. In a large bowl, cream butter & 3 cups sugar. Mix in eggs, mashed bananas, sour cream, vanilla & cinnamon. Mix in salt, baking soda & flour. Stir in nuts. Divide into prepared pans. Bake for 1 hour, until a toothpick inserted in center comes out clean.

Best Ever Lemon Scones
Annie Laurie Cisneros from Joy of the Repast: Favorite Recipes of Family and Friends

3 cups flour
2 1/2 tsp. baking powder
1/3 cups sugar
I lemon (zest only)
3/4 cups butter
1 cup buttermilk (or plain yogurt)
1/4 cups raisins, dried cherries or cranberries (cut into pieces)
1 cup confectioners sugar
1 tbsp lemon juice
lemon zest

Cut together the butter, sugar, baking powder, and lemon zest. The butter should be cut into the size of a pea or even a little larger. Add the buttermilk and dried fruit; handle the dough as little as possible. Turn dough on a floured surface and knead gently a few times. Press dough into a circle (about 1/2 or more inch high) and then cut into wedges. Place wedges on parchment paper lined baking sheet (or a well greased pan). Bake at 425 degrees for 15 minutes or a golden brown. When cooled, glaze with a powdered sugar and lemon juice & zest icing. (about 1 cup confectioners sugar, 1 tbsp. lemon juice, and lemon zest)

Biscuits (quick and easy)
Aunt Evelyn (Grandpa Bennett's sister) from Grandma Bennett's recipes

1 1/2 cups self rising flour
1/3 cups cooking oil
2/3 cup milk

Stir together with fold. Pat out to desired thickness. Cut biscuits and Bake 450° or 500° until brown.

Breolotti
Marion Bennett from Bennett's & Beyond: A Family Cookbook

1 pkg dry yeast
1/4 c warm water
4 c flour
1/4 c sugar
1 1/2 tsp salt
1/2 c hot water
1/2 c milk
1/4 c softened butter
1 egg
1 lb bulk sausage
1 c onion (chopped fine)
1 1/2 c grated Cheddar cheese

Grease cookie sheet. In a large bowl dissolve yeast in warm water; add 2 cups flour, sugar, salt, water, milk, butter, and egg. With electric mixer, blend at low speed until moistened. Beat 2 minutes at medium speed. By hand, stir in remaining flour to form a stiff dough; cover and let rise in warm place until light and doubled in size, 45 to 60 minutes.

To prepare filling, brown sausage in skillet with the chopped onion; pour off excess fat.

When dough has doubled in size, stir down and place on a floured surface. Knead until no longer sticky. Roll out to an 18 x 12 inch rectangle, then cut lengthwise into three 18 x 4 inch strips. Spread each with the sausage and onion mixture; sprinkle each with the grated cheese.

Beginning with the 18 inch side, roll up each strip; seal edges and ends. On the prepared cookie sheet, braid the three rolls together; cover and allow to rise until doubled, about 45 to 60 minutes. Bake in a 350° oven 30 to 35 minutes, or until golden brown. Serve warm or cool.

Broccoli Cornbread

Dawn-Marie Sneed, compliments of Chris LeBoeuf from Dawn-Marie's Favorite Family and Cookbook Recipes

2 boxes of Jiffy Corn Muffin Mix
3 Eggs
8 oz. cottage cheese (small curd)
1 c. cheddar cheese (grated)
1/2 c. butter or margarine
1/4 c. chopped onion
3/4 c. milk
10 oz. frozen chopped broccoli, thawed and drained

Melt butter in 9" x 13" baking dish. Mix corn muffin mix, eggs, cottage cheese, cheddar cheese, onion and milk in bowl. Make sure broccoli is well-drained and pat dry.

Add broccoli to other ingredients in bowl and stir. Pour contents of bowl into baking dish; mix lightly with the melted butter/margarine. Bake in 350° oven for 35-40 minutes, until golden brown.

Company French Toast

Berna Andreachi from The Vold Family Cookbook Project

1/2 c. butter
3/4 c. brown sugar
12 slices English muffin bread
6 eggs
1 2/3 c. milk
Sugar
Cinnamon
1/2 - 1 c. blueberries

Melt butter in 9x13 in. pan. Put in brown sugar. Put bread in pan stacked 2 deep. Mix eggs and milk. Pour over bread. Sprinkle with sugar and cinnamon. Sprinkle blueberries on top. Put in refrigerator covered. Bake at 350° 45 min. uncovered.

Cranberry Nut Bread

Nancy Atwell from Four Generations of Johnson Women

Group 1 ~
2 cups flour
1 1/2 t baking powder
1/2 t baking soda
3/4 cup sugar
1/2 t salt

Group 2~
1/2 cup orange juice
1 orange rind, grated
3 T butter
2 T hot water
1 egg, beaten

Group 3 ~
1 cup cranberries, cut in half
1/2 cup nuts, chopped fine (walnuts are good)

Combine group 1 in a small mixing bowl. Set aside. Lightly mix group 2 in a large mixing bowl. Add Group 1 and beat lightly. Then add cranberries and nuts. Careful, too much beating will cause large holes in the dough.

Pour into 1 large or several small loaf pans. Fill pan(s) about 3/4 full.

Bake at 350° for 40 to 60 minutes or until brown (time is dependent on size of pan). For several loaves, rearrange mid-way through baking time. Not recommended to use multiple shelves as browning is never quite right. Breads should be firm but moist on top.

Crawfish Bread

Allie Bourgeois from The Tasty Bourgeois Cookbook

2 cups peeled crawfish tails
1 loaf French bread
1/2 stick butter
1/2 cup diced onions
1/2 cup diced celery
1/4 cup diced red bell peppers
1 tbsp minced garlic
1/2 tsp Dijon mustard
1/2 cup mayonnaise
1/3 cup Mozzarella cheese
1/3 cup Cheddar cheese

Slice French bread in half lengthwise and scoop out the inside of the loaf. Set aside. In a large skillet, melt butter over medium-high heat. Sauté crawfish, onions, celery, bell peppers and garlic 15 minutes. Blend in mustard and mayonnaise. Add cheeses and blend until melted. Spread crawfish mixture inside the bread then put halves back together. Butter the top of the loaf, wrap it in foil and bake on a barbecue pit or in a 350°F oven for 20–30 minutes. Cut bread into slices and serve hot.

Crawfish Cornbread

Harriet Duhe' Melancon from A Taste of Our Family

1 pound crawfish tails
2 cups yellow cornmeal
3 eggs
1 can cream style corn
1 1/2 cup cheddar cheese, grated
3/4 cup onion tops
2 jalapeno peppers, finely chopped
1 onion, finely chopped
1/2 cup bell peppers, finely chopped
1/2 tsp baking soda
1 tsp salt
1/2 cup oil
3 tsp baking powder
1 cup milk

Saute onions and bell pepper in a small amount of butter until the onions are clear. Add jalapeno peppers and set aside. Mix together all other ingredients, except crawfish. Add in cooked onions and peppers. Then stir in crawfish.
Pour into a lightly greased 13x9 inch pan and bake in a 400° oven for 35 to 40 minutes.

German Brown Bread

Renee' Bowers Bundy from Home Sweet Home Recipes

8 oz. pitted dates
2 tsp. baking soda
2 c. boiling water
2 Tbsp. butter
2 c. sugar
2 eggs
2 tsp. vanilla
4 c. flour
1 Tbsp. salt
1 c. chopped nuts

Cut up dates and mix with baking soda. Pour boiling water over dates and let stand while mixing the remaining ingredients. Cream butter, eggs, vanilla and sugar. Combine flour and salt. Add flour mixture to creamed mixture alternately with date mixture. Mix well. Add nuts. Pour into greased loaf pan and bake at 325° for 1 hour and 20 minutes.

This bread first caught my attention because of its unusual shape. Years ago the bread was baked in large metal soup cans and I loved its round cylinder shape. Not being a fan of dates, I was hesitant to sample a slice and did so only to be polite. Now I look forward to this bread every year on Thanksgiving and Christmas Eve. This bread freezes well.

Ginny's Award Winning Irish Soda Bread

Ginny Larkin from The New Donovan Family Cookbook Volume II

3 cups all-purpose flour
1 cup whole wheat flour
1 ½ tsp. baking soda
1 tsp. salt
4 tbl. sugar
1 ½ tbl. caraway seeds
1 cup raisins or currants
1 ¾ cups well-shaken buttermilk
1 tbl. unsalted butter, melted

Preheat oven to 375 degree. Butter and flour a large baking sheet, shaking off excess flour. Sift together flour, baking soda, and salt into a large bowl. Stir in sugar, caraway seeds, and raisins. Add buttermilk and stir just until dough is evenly moistened but still lumpy.

Transfer dough to a well-floured surface and gently knead with floured hands about 8 times to form a soft but slightly less sticky ball. Halve dough and form into 2 balls.

Pat out each ball into a domed 6-inch round on baking sheet. Cut a ½ inch deep X onto each loaf with a sharp knife, then brush with butter.

Bake in middle of oven until golden brown and bottom sounds hollow when tapped about 35-40 minutes. Transfer loaves to rack to cool completely.

Grandma Stella's Zucchini Pineapple Bread

Nancy Alvord from Family Recipes To Remember

3 Eggs
1 cup salad Oil
2 cups Sugar
2 tsp. Vanilla
2 cups shredded Zucchini
1-8oz. crushed Pineapple
3 cups Flour
2 tsp. Baking Soda
1 tsp. Salt
1/2 tsp. Baking Powder
1 1/2 tsp. Cinnamon
3/4 tsp. Nutmeg
1 cup chopped Walnuts
1 cup Raisins

Beat the eggs, add oil, sugar and vanilla. Beat until thick and foamy. Stir in zucchini and pineapple. Combine the dry ingredients. Add to mixer. Stir in nuts and raisins. Pour into 2 bread loaf pans that have been greased or pam'd. Bake at 350° for 1 hour.

Holiday Bread

Gloria Cody from All My Children Gotta Eat

3 c. flour
2 c. sugar
1 tsp. baking soda
1 tsp. salt
1 tsp. cinnamon
3 eggs
1 1/2 c. vegetable oil
1 c. chopped walnuts or pecans
1 c. coconut
3 ripe bananas, mashed
1 large can crushed pineapple, drained
1 1/2 tsp. vanilla

Preheat oven to 350º. Mix first 5 ingredients. Add eggs and oil. Add remaining 5 ingredients. Pour into 2 greased and floured loaf pans. Bake for 1 hour to 1 hour and 15 minutes.

Home Ec Coffeecake

Nancy Register from Family Favorites

1 c flour
1 T sugar
2 t baking powder
1 egg (beaten
2 T oil
1/2 c milk
cinnamon & brown sugar to taste

Put dry ingredients into bowl and mix well. Add wet ingredients and stir 4-6 times. Pour into greased 8 ' cake pan. Sprinkle cinnamon and brown sugar over top.Bake at 400 degrees for 20 minutes.

Jordan Marsh Blueberry Muffins

Karon Davenport Nason 1954 from The Whitcher Family Descendants Cookbook

8 tbsp (1 stick) soft unsalted butter
1 1/4 cups sugar
1/2 teaspoon salt
2 large eggs
2 cups all-purpose bleached flour
2 teaspoons baking powder
1/2 cup buttermilk or milk
1 pint blueberries, rinsed, drained and dried

One 12-cavity muffin pan with paper liners.
1. Set a rack in the middle of the oven and preheat to 375 degrees F.
2. Cream the butter with the sugar and salt by hand or with an electric mixer until light. Beat in the eggs, one at a time, until smooth. Mix the flour and baking powder together well and stir into the batter alternating with the buttermilk.
3. Crush a quarter of the berries and stir into the batter; fold in the remaining berries whole.
4. Spoon the batter into the muffin pan. Sprinkle the tops with some sugar.
5. Bake the muffins about 30 minutes, until well risen and deep golden. Cool the muffins in the pan.

La Jolla French Toast

Karen Christiansen from The Kearney Family Cookbook

1 loaf soft French bread
1 qt. whipping cream
10 eggs
3/4 cup lemonade concentrate
1/2 cup sugar
Pinch of salt
2 tbsp. vanilla
3 tbsp. lemon extract
Butter for grilling
Powdered sugar

Slice French bread diagonally about 1 1/2-inch thick. Combine eggs, cream, lemonade, sugar, salt, vanilla and lemon extract. Pour over bread slices. Cover and refrigerate overnight. Remove bread, discard liquid. Spread butter on griddle. Cook bread on grill until golden brown on both sides. Bake in a 450 degree oven for 5 to 7 minutes or until bread is puffed up like a souffle. Dust with powdered sugar. Serves 6 to 8.

Orange Pineapple Bread

Georgia Perry - WalMart from The Toledo Area Chapter APA Celebrates National Payroll Week!

1 small can chunk pineapple
2 c pitted prunes/dates
1 jar of orange jam
1/2 boiling water
1/3 c honey
2 egg whites
1 t vanilla
1 c whole wheat flour
1 c cake flour
1 t baking soda
1/4 t salt

Preheat oven to 325° Boil water and put in prunes/dates. Turn down to a simmer, place lid on pot & set aside. Combine orange jam, honey, egg whites & vanilla. Take dates out of steaming water & combine with the above mixture. Add pineapples. Sift flour, soda & salt. Add the orange mixture to the flour mixture. Fill 2 bread loaf pans half full. Bake for 30 minutes or until toothpick comes out clean.

Phil's Garlic Cheese Bread

Phil Slessor from 'We Love You Alison' Cookbook

1 Stick of Margarine
1 Jar of Craft Old English Sharp Cheddar cheese
Garlic powder to taste.
1 loaf French Bread

Whip margarine, cheese and garlic powder in mixer until fully integrated. Slice bread length wise spread liberally with cheese mixture. Slice down into loaf about every inch and a half but not all the way through just partially the way through. Place under broiler on high heat until nice and toasted.

Pumpkin or Banana Bread with Diced Apples

Stephanie Osler from The Wiersch Family Cookbook

3 1/2 c. flour
2 tsp. baking soda
1 1/2 tsp. salt
1 tsp. cinnamon
1 tsp. nutmeg
3 cups sugar
1 cup vegetable oil
4 eggs
2/3 c. water
2 c. canned pumpkin
1/2 c. finely diced apple
1 c. pecans, chopped (optional)

Preheat oven to 350. Sift together all ingredients from flour to sugar and make a well. Then add all the ingredients from oil to apple. Mix until smooth and pour into 3 greased and floured loaf pans. Bake 50 minutes to one hour.

Raspberry Cheese Coffee Cake

Amy and Sarah Hollister from McKee Cooks

8 oz. cream cheese, softened
1/2 c. butter or margarine, softened
1 c. sugar
2 lg. eggs
1/4 c. milk
1/2 t. vanilla extract
1 3/4 c. flour
1 t. baking powder
1/2 t. baking soda
1/4 t. salt
1/2 c. seedless raspberry preserves
3 T. powdered sugar

Beat first 3 ingredients with electric mixer on medium. Add eggs, milk, vanilla; beat until smooth. Mix flour and next 3 ingredients; add to cream cheese mix; beat on low until well blended. Spread into greased/floured 13x9 pan. Dollop with preserves; swirl with knife. Bake at 350° for 30 minutes as cake begins to leave sides of pan. Cool; sprinkle with powdered sugar. Cut into squares.

Sour Milk Doughnuts

Ann L. Richardson from The Richardson Family Cookbook

4 c. flour, enriched
2 t. baking powder
1/2 t. baking soda
1 t. salt
1/4 t. nutmeg
1/2 t. cinnamon
2 T. shortening
1 c. sugar
2 eggs
1 c. sour milk or buttermilk
Sift together flour, baking powder, baking soda, salt, nutmeg and cinnamon. Set aside. Cream shortening. Add

sugar gradually and beat until light and fluffy. Add eggs one at a time, beating well after each addition. Add sifted dry ingredients and milk alternately, stirring until well blended. Roll out 1/2" thick, cut and let stand uncovered 20 minutes. Drop into hot fat and fry until golden brown. Sprinkle with sugar, powdered sugar or glaze with powdered sugar icing, if desired.

Southwest Green Chili Corn Bread

Diane Erickson from The Zuelke Family Cookbook

1 c. butter
3/4 c. sugar
4 eggs
1/2 c. green chilis, diced
1 1/2 c. creamed corn
1/2 c. cheddar cheese, shredded
1/2 c. Jack cheese, shredded
1 c. flour
1 c. yellow corn meal
2 T. baking powder
1 tsp. salt

Preheat oven to 325°
Cream butter and sugar. Add eggs slowly, one at a time. Add remaining ingredients and mix until well incorporated. Pour into a well buttered 9 inch square pan. Bake for 1 hour.

Sticky Buns

Sandra Perales from McMillan Family and Friends Cookbook

1 1/4 Cup Milk
1/2 Cup warm water
2 pkgs. active dry yeast
2 eggs
5 1/2 to 6 Cups regular flour, sifted
1/2 Cup margarine
2 tsp. Sugar
1/2 Cup Sugar
Brown Sugar
Cinnamon
Walnut pieces (optional)
Raisins (optional)

Heat and cool milk to lukewarm. Melt margarine and cool to lukewarm. In a large mixing bowl, dissolve yeast in lukewarm water. Add lukewarm milk and 2 tsp sugar. Set aside for 5 minutes.

Sift flour into a large bowl and make a hollow in center, add 1/2 cup sugar, salt, cooled butter, and eggs. Next add yeast. Combine ingredients using a wooden spoon or dough hook of an electric mixer. If using an electric mixer, begin on the lowest setting to blend and then adjust to high for 5 minutes. Should the dough become sticky, add a little more flour; the dough must remain moderately soft. Knead for 5 minutes on a lightly floured board. Let rest for 5 minutes.

Place dough in a greased bowl; turn once to grease lightly. Cover bowl, place in a warm, area for 1 1/2 hours or until doubled in bulk. Punch dough down and turn out onto a lightly floured board and roll out in a large rectangle.

Carefully cover with 1/2 Cup melted butter or margarine; next sprinkle generously with brown sugar, then cinnamon. If desired you may also sprinkle with nuts and raisins. Roll up like a jelly roll and cut into 1 inch pieces.

Bread and Muffins

Prepare your 9x13 pan by melting 1/2 cup butter or margarine and covering the bottom of the pan. Next sprinkle brown sugar over the bottom of the pan . You may also drizzle maple syrup or honey over brown sugar.

Finally place cut rolls in pan. Cover and let rise about 20 minutes in a warm draft-free place. Bake at 375° for 15 to 20 minutes or until rolls are golden brown. Turn rolls out onto wax paper to cool.

Swedish Rye Bread

Naomi Jones from The Jones-Simpson Cookbook

2 pkgs. Yeast
5 cups luke warm water
1 cup molasses
1 tbsp. salt
1 tbsp. lard
1/2 tsp. anise seed
4 cups rye flour
6 cups white flour

Mix in large bowl and knead for 10 minutes. Put in greased bowl and let rise till double in bulk. Punch down, let rest 10 minutes & make into loaves. Let rise again. Bake 375° for 35 minutes. Makes 4 - 1 1/2 lb. loaves.

Personal Notes: A variation of this is to use 1/2 cup oil in place of the lard.

Traditional Irish Soda Bread

Wendy Lotze from Favorite Recipes

1 lb plain flour (about 4 c.)
1 1/2 c. buttermilk
1 tsp. baking soda
1 tsp. salt

Mix together the dry ingredients, making sure there are no lumps in the soda. Add the buttermilk and mix well with a wooden spoon. Knead lightly on a floured surface. Form into a round loaf and place on a baking sheet. Using a wet knife, score the top with a cross. Bake at the top of a hot oven (350°) for 45 minutes, until the bottom of the loaf sounds hollow when rapped with the knuckle.

Twyla Palmer's Mini Cinnamon Rolls

Nita Orndorff from Grammy's Family Cookbook

1 can refrigerated crescent rolls
2 Tbsp margarine, softened
2 Tbsp sugar
1/2 tsp cinnamon
nuts optional
3/4 c powdered sugar
1 Tbsp milk

Preheat oven to 350°. Unroll crescent dough into one large rectangle. Seal perforations. Spread margarine evenly over dough. Combine sugar and cinnamon. Sprinkle evenly over dough. Sprinkle nuts over sugar cinnamon mixture. Roll up rectangle tightly, starting from longest side. Cut roll into 20 - 24 slices.

Bake for 20 to 25 minutes. Mix powered sugar and milk for glaze (or use 1/2 c Vanilla Frosting, melted). Glaze warm rolls.

Yorkshire Pudding

Brenda Neroni from A Fine Collection of Yum

4 eggs
2 cups all-purpose flour
2 cups milk
1/4 cup vegetable oil

Preheat the oven to 450 degrees F. In a large bowl, whisk together the eggs and milk and salt until well blended. Whisk in the flour one cup at a time until frothy and well blended.
Set aside. Distribute the oil equally among 12 deep muffin cups, a little over a teaspoon per cup. Place in the oven for 5 to 10 minutes, until smoking. Remove from the oven and quickly ladle about 1/4 cup of batter into each cup. It's important that they are hot and smokey. Bake for 30 to 35 minutes in the preheated oven. Serve immediately.

Zucchini Bread

Kathy Schew from Trickey Pond Family Reunion Cookbook

4 eggs
2 1/2 cups sugar
1 1/2 cups oil
2 Tbsp. vanilla
3 cups zucchini
2 tsp. cinnamon
2 tsp. salt
2 tsp. baking soda
1/2 tsp baking powder
4 1/2 cups flour
1 cup chopped nuts (optional)

Shred or blend zucchini. Mix all ingredients well. Pour into 2 greased and floured loaf pans. Bake at 350° for one hour or until done.

Soups, Stews
Salads and Sauces

Hearty Vegetable Stew pg. 61

Cajun Chicken Caesar Salad pg. 52

Chicken & Wild Rice Soup pg. 53

Bed Side Stew

Joanne Bahl from Family Favorites

2 lbs. stewing beef cubes
3 potatoes (cut into quarters)
1/2 bunch carrots cut up
2 onions
11/2 bay leaves
1/2 pkg frozen peas
1 can tomato soup

Mix all ingredients and put into casserole dish.
Pour tomato soup over mixture. *Do not stir.
Cover. Bake in 225° oven for 4 hours. It makes its own gravy. **Do not brown beef cubes.

Blue cheese spread

Catherine Jeansonne from The Jeansonne Family Cookbook Project

1/2 lb (8 oz) cream cheese
1/4 lb blue cheese
1 T dairy sour cream
1 tsp freeze dried chopped chives

Break up cheeses: place in blender or small bowl of electric mixer with remaining ingredients. Blend or whip until smooth and creamy.

Brazilian Black Bean Soup

Annie Laurie Cisneros from Joy of the Repast: Favorite Recipes of Family and Friends

2 cup dry black beans
6 cups water
1 tbs. olive oil
3 - 4 cups chopped onion
1 medium carrot chopped
1 medium bell pepper chopped
10 medium cloves garlic, chopped
2 medium tomatoes diced
3 tbs cumin
2 tsp. salt
1 & 1/2 cup orange juice
black pepper to taste

Wash the beans and soak them covered for 4 hours or overnight. Drain and add 4 cups water and salt. Bring to a boil and then simmer, covered, for 1 1/2 hours. (Better to use a pressure cooker, cooking for approximately 30 min.)

Sauté in olive oil the onions, garlic, bell pepper, carrot, and cumin (best with freshly ground cumin seeds - toast the seeds before grinding). Cook until vegetables are soft. Add veggies to the cooked beans and let simmer for about 30 minutes. Stir in orange juice, black pepper and optional tomatoes.

Cover and cook 10 to 20 more minutes. Taste and make adjustments. Puree all or some of the soup in a blender or food processor.

Cajun Chicken Cesar Salad

Melinda Carreon from My Grandma's Kitchen

4 chicken breasts
2 bags of chopped Romaine lettuce
1 bag garlic butter croutons
Marie's Creamy Cesar Salad Dressing
1 c olive oil
1 c coarsely chopped red onion
Shredded fresh Parmesan cheese
Cajun Choice seasoning

Wash and dry the chicken breasts. Place in a dish and pour olive oil on top. Make sure chicken is covered with olive oil (If you need to add more olive oil you can). Sprinkle Cajun Choice seasoning generously over chicken. Cover and refrigerate (you can leave the chicken in the refrigerator for 15 minutes or several hours).

Grill chicken on the barbecue on medium heat for 7 minutes. Flip chicken over and sprinkle generously with the Cajun Choice seasoning. Cook chicken for another 7 minutes or until no longer pink. Remove chicken from grill and slice chicken into thin slices.

Put lettuce, onions and chicken into a large serving bowl. Add dressing and Parmesan cheese to taste. Serve immediately.

Cheese Ball

Terry Wasson from The Wasson Family Cookbook Project

2-8 oz cream cheese
1 small crushed pineapple-drained
1 Tbsp. Lawry's Seasoning
2 Tbsp. green pepper
Chopped pecans and parsley

Mix all ingredients together except pecans and parsley. Form into cheese ball and roll in pecans and parsley. Refrigerate.

Cheeseburger Soup

Jane Burke from Aelred and Rita Wagner Family Cookbook

1/2 pound ground beef
3/4 cup chopped onion
3/4 cup shredded carrots
3/4 cup diced celery
1 teaspoon dried basil
1 teaspoon dried parsley flakes
4 tablespoons butter
3 cups chicken broth
4 cups diced peeled potatoes
1/4 cup all purpose flour
1-1/2 cups milk
3/4 teaspoon salt
1/2 teaspoon pepper
8 ounces processed American cheese block - cubed (2 cups)

Start with a 3 quart saucepan and brown the beef and drain off the grease and set off to the side. Using the same pan saute with 1 tablespoon butter the onions, carrots, celery, basil and parsley until tender. This will be about 10 minutes. Add broth, potatoes and beef and bring to a boil. Reduce heat to simmer, cover and gently cook for about 12 minutes. Make sure the potatoes are tender. In a small skillet melt the butter. Add flour and cook while stirring for about 4 minutes or until mixture is bubbly. Add this to the soup. Bring to a boil and stir for about 2 minutes. Reduce to low heat. Add the cheese, milk, salt and pepper. Stir until all the cheese melts. Remove from heat.

Chicken & Broccoli Alfredo

Joyce Van Sessen from The Van Sessen Family Cookbook Project

8 oz. pkg. linguine, uncooked
1 cup broccoli flowers
2 Tablespoon butter
10 3/4 oz. can cream of mushroom soup
1/2 cup milk
1/2 cup grated Parmesan cheese
1/4 teaspoon pepper
1 lb. package. boneless skinless chicken breasts, cubed

Cook linguine according to package directions; add broccoli during the Last 4 mins.of cooking time. Drain; set aside. Heat butter in a 12' skillet; add chicken, Heat until juices run clear when chicken is pierced with a fork; reduce heat. Stir in soup, milk, cheese, pepper and linguine mixture; heat through.

Chicken & Wild Rice Soup

Michiele Ward from The Ward/Bagley/Blevins and Friends Family Cookbook

2 cups uncooked wild rice
2 cups cooked and cut up chicken
1 chicken bullion cube
2 or 3 cups milk
garlic, onion and salt to taste
1 can cream of chicken or mushroom soup

Cook rice in rice cooker. Add bullion cube as it cooks. If no rice cooker, boil in a pan. When rice is finished cooking, add chicken, soup and milk. Heat and serve. I add a can of mushrooms too.

Chicken Tortellini Chowder

Kelly Champlin Church from Lewis Girl's Lucky Duck Cookbook

2 boneless chicken breasts
2 garlic cloves
3 Tbs. butter
2 c. chicken broth
1 tsp. cumin
2 c. half and half
2 c. shredded Monterey Jack cheese
1 can cream style corn
1- 4 oz. can of chopped green chiles, undrained
1 tsp. hot pepper sauce
1 pkg. fresh or frozen tortellini

Cut chicken into bite size pieces. Brown chicken in garlic & butter until chicken is no longer pink. Add broth to pan w/ cumin; bring to a boil. Cook tortellini as directed. Reduce heat of the broth, cover & simmer. Add cream, cheese, chiles, tortellini & hot sauce. Cook & stir until cheese is melted.

Chicken-Tortilla Soup

Robin Gordon from The Gordon/Schorr Family Cookbook Project

1 T olive oil
1 cup chopped onion
2 garlic cloves, minced
2 cups shredded cooked chicken breast
1 cup frozen whole-kernel corn
1/4 cup dry white wine
1 T chopped seeded jalapeno pepper
1 t ground cumin
1 t Worcestershire sauce
1/2 T chili powder
2 (14 1/4-ounce) cans chicken broth
1 (14.5 oz) can diced peeled tomatoes, undrained
1 can condensed tomato soup
1 1/4 cups crushed unsalted baked tortilla chips
1/2 cup fat-free sour cream

Heat oil in a Dutch oven over medium-high heat. Add onion and garlic; sauté 2 minutes. Stir in chicken and next 9 ingredients (chicken through tomato soup); bring to a boil. Reduce heat, and simmer 1 hour. Ladle soup into bowls; top with tortilla chips and sour cream.

Cioppino

Brenda Neroni from A Fine Collection of Yum

1/4 cup of olive oil
1 lg onion, chopped
1 green bell pepper -- seeded and chopped
3 cloves garlic -- minced
½ cp finely chopped parsley
1 tsp dried basil
½ tsp dried oregano
28 oz can Italian plum tomatoes, chopped
6 oz can of tomato paste
2 c dry red or white wine
1 bottle of clam juice
1 tsp salt
¼ tsp cracked pepper
1 lb of monk fish or haddock fillets -- cut in pieces
1 8 oz. lobster tail, cut in pieces
2 lb lump crab meat
1 lb. of mussels, shelled or in shells
1 lb Shrimp, 40 to 50 count-- shelled and de-veined,
2 cans of whole baby clams, or 24 little neck clams in shells
2 cans of premium chunk white tuna
1 lb of small bay scallops

1. In a deep, heavy, large kettle or Dutch oven, heat olive oil over medium heat. Add onion, garlic, and bell pepper. Cook, stirring often, until onion is soft but not browned. Mix in parsley, basil, and oregano. Stir in tomatoes and their liquid, clam juice, tomato paste, wine, salt, and pepper.

2. Bring to a boil, cover, reduce heat, and simmer for 1 hour. Uncover and boil gently, stirring occasionally, over medium-low heat until sauce is fairly thick (30 to 35 minutes).

3. Cube and add seafood, fresh fish first, then shell fish, then clams and tuna last. Heat through until shrimp and lobster are just pink and keep on a low flame covered for 20 more minutes.

Cold Black Bean Salad

Nancy Bridges from The Jones-Simpson Cookbook

1 can black beans, rinsed and drained
1 can chick peas, rinsed and drained
2 fresh onion; chopped
2-4 chopped Roma tomatoes, drained
1 avocado, chopped
1 mango, chopped (may use frozen)
2 Tbsp. fresh cilantro
Small amount chopped jalapeno pepper
Juice of 1 lime

Mix all ingredients and chill. Serve plain or over bed of lettuce.

Corn and Red Bell Pepper Chowder with Kielbasa

2007 Minnesota Aharts' Cookbook from 2008 Ahart Family Reunion Cookbook

1/2 lb kielbasa sausage
1 cup chopped yellow onion
2 cloves garlic, minced
1 cup chopped red pepper
1/2 Tbsp olive oil, if needed
2 cups chicken broth or stock
1/2 tsp salt
1/8 tsp white pepper
1 1/2 cups corn kernels, fresh or frozen
1 cup half and half
1/4 cup chopped parsley
3 medium red potatoes (about 1 lb), unpeeled, cubed

Cut kielbasa into 3/8-inch slices and then halved. In a large Dutch oven over medium heat, combine kielbasa sausage, chopped yellow onion, garlic, and red pepper and saute until vegetables are tender, 6 to 7 minutes. Add oil, if needed. Add stock, potatoes, salt, and white pepper. Bring to a boil. Reduce heat to medium-low and cook, covered, until potatoes are tender, about 20 minutes. Add corn, half and half, and parsley and simmer, uncovered until flavors are blended, about 10 minutes longer. Enjoy with warm crusty bread!

Cornbread Salad

Donna Riser from Southern Family Cookbook Project

1 box Jiffy corn muffin mix
1 egg
1/3 cup milk
4 tomatoes peeled and chopped
1 green pepper chopped
1 med. onion, chopped
9 slices bacon, cooked and crumbled
1 cup mayonnaise
1/4 cup sweet pickle juice

Mix corn muffin mix, egg and milk. Bake 400° for 15-20 min. Cool, crumble and put 1/2 of mixture in 9x13 pan. Combine tomatoes, peppers, onions, and bacon. Toss and put 1/2 of mixture in layer over bread. Mix mayo and pickle juice. Put 1/2 of mixture over tomato mixture. Repeat layers. Make several layers. Make several hours before serving.

Cottonwood Chili

Jean Thayer from Memories of Love, Cooking and Great Smells!

1 lb. lean ground sirloin
1 lb. lean ground buffalo
1 lb. lean pork cubes
2 cans Bush's Best chili beans
2 cans chili-seasoned diced tomatoes
1 lg. can diced tomatoes
2 small cans diced Hatch chilies
1 chopped onion
4-5 minced garlic cloves
Chili power to taste
1 - 2 Tbsp. cumin to taste

Brown meats together in a large pot. Add remaining ingredients and simmer for 2-3 hours or more.

Cranberry-Cream Cheese Salad

Marie Bateman from 'We Love You Alison' Cookbook

1 - 6 oz package Cherry Jello
2 c boiling water
2 large apples, peeled and grated
1/2 c chopped pecans
16 oz can whole Cranberry Sauce
8 oz package Cream Cheese (softened)
1 c powdered sugar
1 lb 4 oz can crushed pineapple (drained)
8 oz package Cool Whip

Jello Base - Dissolve cherry Jello in boiling water. Cool slightly. Add apples, chopped pecans and cranberry sauce. Pour into a 13x9 inch glass dish and refrigerate until firm.

While jello is firming make Cream Cheese Topping. Blend cream cheese and Cool Whip until smooth. Add powdered sugar, then crushed pineapple. Stir all ingredients until smooth.

After jello is firm, spoon cream cheese topping over top of jello, spreading evenly. Sprinkle with additional 1/4 c chopped pecans.

Cover and chill overnight or until well set.

Cream of Potato Soup W/O Corn

Suzanne Dunscomb from Bennett's & Beyond: A Family Cookbook

5 - 6 large potatoes, cut up
1 medium onion, minced
1 lg can evaporated milk
6 c. water
2 tsp. salt
1/4 tsp. cayenne pepper
1/2 tsp. ground black pepper {optional}
1 bag frozen corn {optional}

Boil potatoes and onion until tender in salted water. Once tender, mash potatoes, leaving them in the potato water, then add milk, seasoning and corn {if desired}. Blend thoroughly and serve hot. Approximately. 2 qts.

Creamed Broccoli Soup

Barbara Mothershead from Mom's Favorite Recipes

1 pkg frozen chopped broccoli
1/2 c. celery, finely chopped
2 Tbs onion, finely chopped
1/4 c. butter or margarine
1/4 c. flour
1 1/2 c. milk
1 14oz can chicken broth
1/4 t. pepper
1/4 t. celery salt
1/2 c. ham, finely chopped
1/2 c. shredded cheddar cheese

Cook broccoli according to package directions only until thawed, drain well. Saute celery and onions in butter until tender,. Stir in flour, add milk, and broth; heat and stir until thickened and smooth. Add seasonings and drained broccoli and ham. Simmer 10 minutes, stir frequently, add cheese and stir until melted.

Creamy Rich Corn Chowder

Patricia Thrasher-Waller from The Thrasher Family Cookbook Project

5 slices bacon, diced
1 large onion, chopped
2 medium potatoes, cubed
2 c. chicken broth
1-1/2 c. fresh corn kernels, cut from cob
1 tsp. salt
1/2 tsp. black pepper
2 cups half & half

Cook bacon until crisp. Remove bacon and reserve. In the bacon drippings, saute' onion until tender. Add potatoes and broth. Cover and simmer until potatoes are barely tender. Add the corn, salt, and pepper. Continue to simmer 10-15 minutes longer. Stir in the cream and heat just till boiling. Sprinkle with reserved bacon.

Crockpot Split Pea Soup

Melissa Martin from The Martin Family Cookbook

1 lb. green split peas
1 large carrot, chopped
2 stalks celery, chopped
1 large onion, chopped
2 T. dried parsley
1 T. salt
1 T. Worcestershire sauce
1 ham hock

Put all ingredients in slow cooker. Cover with water, three inches over the ingredients. Cook all day on high. Remove bones from ham hock. Serve hot.

Soups, Stews, Salads and Sauces

Cucumber Salad

Vara Wallace from A Real Southern Comfort

1 large cucumber
1/2 cup rice vinegar
2 tbsp water
1 tbsp sugar
1/4 tsp. salt
dash white pepper
2 tbsp dill weed
1 medium onion sliced

Peel and thinly slice the cucumber. Place with the sliced onion into a bowl and sprinkle with vinegar, water, sugar, salt, pepper and dill. Chill for at least 2 hours.

Debe's Apricot Salad

Milly Noah from Grits to Gourmet

4 1/2 cups(3 cans) apricot nectar
1 cup canned apricot halves
4 packages plain gelatin
3/4 cup sugar
2 cans pitted bing cherries
1/2 cup lemon juice
3/4 tsp. salt
3 cups extra fruit (bananas, apples, cantalope, canned peaches, drained, or honeydew).

Drain apricots and puree; save juice and add to nectar if needed. Soften gelatin in lemon juice. Add sugar and salt to nectar and heat until sugar dissolves. Add softened gelatin to hot nectar to dissolve, then cool. Add pureed apricots. Pour into large, greased bundt pan or ring mold and chill until slightly set. Add cherries and other fruit. Chill until set.

Frances Picante Sauce

Frances Hanson, wife of Dean Hanson from Hanson Family Cookbook

1 large can tomatoes
2 tsp. salt
1/4 tsp. garlic powder
1/8 oz. cilantro
2 or 3 jalapeños
1/2 small onion
1 green pepper

Put everything in blender and chop. Ready to serve.

Fresh Tomato and Ginger Soup

Paulette Hackman from Our Great Family

2 lbs. tomatoes, quartered;
garlic, one clove minced;
ginger, fresh, about 1-inch, chopped;
1/2 red pepper, chopped;
1 good-sized shallot, minced;
1/2 carrot, chopped;
1/2 t crushed mint
1 can of chicken or vegetable stock
1/2 c water
salt and pepper to taste

To roast the fresh tomato quarters, toss all of them in a bowl with salt and fresh ground pepper and enough olive oil to make them glossy. Put them in a single layer on a heavy baking sheet and roast in a 400° oven for 1/2 hour. Let them cool.

Saute the other veggies in olive oil until they are softened and light brown (carmelized). Add the stock and cook until the vegetables are tender.

Put the roasted tomatoes through a food mill and add the puree to the veggie pot. Add more stock and the water. Finish by blending, chilling, and garnishing with mint, parsley, tiny bits of crystallized ginger, or a splash of good balsamic vinegar.

Frog's Eye Salad

Pauline Pratt from Memories

1-1/3 cups (8oz.) Ronzoni Acini Pepe, uncooked
1 can (20oz.) pineapple chunks, drained (reserve 1/4 cup juice)
1-3/4 cups milk
1/4 cup sugar
1 pkg. (3.4oz.) vanilla instant pudding
1 can (8oz.) crushed pineapple, drained
2 cans (11oz. each) mandarin orange segments, drained
2 cups frozen non-dairy whipped topping, thawed
3 cups minature marshmallows
1/2 cup flaked coconut

Cook pasta 11 minutes. Rinse with cold water; drain well. In large bowl, beat reserved pineapple juice, milk, sugar, and pudding 2 minutes. Gently stir in pasta and remaining ingredients; cover. Refrigerate at least 5 hours.

Garlic Cream Sauce

Melinda Carreon from My Grandma's Kitchen

1/2 c butter
8 oz sour cream
8 oz heavy whipping cream
1 c parmesan cheese
3 fresh finely chopped garlic cloves

In a medium sized sauce pan slowly melt butter over low heat (Do not let it burn)
While butter is melting, add garlic
Once butter is melted, add sour cream and let that melt, stirring constantly
Once sour cream is melted,add whipping cream

Soups, Stews, Salads and Sauces

Simmer on low heat stirring constantly until warm
Pour over pasta of choice
Add parmesean cheese
Serve

Gary & Carol's Lobster Bisque

Gary Warner from The Warner Family and Friends' Cookbook

1 Lobster (2+lbs)
2 ribs minced Celery
1/2 lb. Butter
1 cup minced onion
2 cups Whole Milk or Half & Half
Reserve 2 cups Lobster broth
2 cups Chicken broth
1 cup Sherry
1/2 cup Flour
1 Tbsp. Tomato Paste
1 Tsp. Worcestershire
Salt & Pepper

Place lobster in a pot of boiling water. Cook 10-15 minutes until lobster is red and cooked. Remove lobster and set aside to cool. Reserve 2 cups of lobster broth for later use.

In a soup pot, melt butter, then saute minced onions and celery until soft and translucent. Add milk or half & half, sherry, chicken broth, salt & pepper to taste. Transfer a cup of hot soup into a small bowl. Whisk in tomato paste and worcestershire. When smoothly combined, return mixture to main soup pot and whisk until combined evenly. In a separate bowl add 2 cups of (hot reserved lobster broth) add 1/2 cup of flour using a whisk. Add flour and lobster broth mixture to soup pot gradually using a whisk. Allow bisque to simmer and the soup will start thickening.

Remove Lobster meat from shell, break or cut meat into smaller pieces and reserve in a seperate bowl. If you prefer a smooth bisque, strain the bisque to remove the onions and celery. Skip this step if you prefer a chowder like texture. Add the lobster meat and allow bisque to simmer (do not boil) for 15 minutes, stirring occasionally.

German Spaetzle (Dumplings)

Eleanor Wark from McMillan Family and Friends Cookbook

1 cup flour
1/4 cup milk
2 eggs
1/2 teaspoon ground nutmeg
1 pinch white pepper
1/2 teaspoon salt
1 gallon hot liquid like chicken broth
2 Tablespoon butter
2 Tablespoon chopped fresh parsley

Mix together flour, salt, white pepper and nutmeg. Beat eggs well and add alternately with the milk to the dry ingredients. Mix until smooth. Press dough through spaetzle maker, or a large holed sieve or metal grater. Drop a few at a time into simmering liquid. Cook 5 to 8 Minutes. Drain well. Saute cooked Spaetzle in butter or margarine. Sprinkle chopped fresh parsley on top, and serve. You can also add these to chicken soup instead of noodles.

Gluten Free Chicken Taco Soup

Sabreena Rabun from The Wellness Cookbook

1 pound shredded or diced chicken
1/2 C. diced onion
1 (15 oz.) can diced tomatoes
1 (8 oz.) can tomato sauce
1 (15 oz.) can red beans, rinsed and drained
1 (17 oz.) can whole kernel corn, with liquid
1 tbsp. chili powder
1 tbsp. cumin powder
1 tbsp. onion powder
3/4 tsp. garlic powder
3/4 tsp. salt
Enough water to make soup

Boil chicken, shred. Put in a large pot. Add all ingredients and water. Bring to a boil. Reduce heat and simmer for 20 minutes. Can add tortilla chips and shredded cheese if you like.

Mix together chili powder, cumin, onion powder, garlic powder and salt for gluten free taco seasoning. Season to taste.

Hearty Vegetable Stew

Helen Burton-McCarthy from McCarthy Family Cookbook

1 1/2 c. chicken stock
1 large onion chopped
3 cloves garlic, minced
1 T. minced fresh ginger root
1 tsp. paprika
1/2 tsp. cinnamon
1/2 tsp. curry powder
1/4 tsp. each salt and pepper
19 oz. can tomatoes
19 oz. can chick peas, drained
2 large potatoes, cut into 1" pieces
2 carrots, thickly sliced
1 sweet red or yellow pepper, seeded,
1 medium zucchini, cut into 1" pieces
1 c. frozen peas
1/4 c. each chopped fresh parsley and coriander

In large flameproof casserole or Dutch oven, combine 1/2 c. chicken stock, onion, garlic, ginger root, paprika, cinnamon, curry powder, salt and pepper. Bring to a boil over high heat. Reduce heat to low; simmer, covered, 5 minutes or until onion is softened. Add tomatoes with their juice, breaking up tomatoes with back of a spoon. Stir in chick-peas, potatoes, carrots, pepper, zucchini, and remaining chicken stock.

Bring to boil over high heat. Reduce heat to medium-low; simmer, covered 25 to 30 minutes or until vegetables are tender. Stir in peas; cook 3 to 5 minutes. Stir in parsley and all but 1 T. of the coriander.

Ladle into wide soup bowls or over a bed of couscous; garnish with reserved coriander. Serve with crusty bread to mop up the juices.

Huckleberry's Chicken Noodle Soup

Brenda Davenport Budreau 1955 from The Whitcher Family Descendants Cookbook

1 large onion, chopped
2 carrots, peeled and chopped
2 celery stalks, sliced
1 garlic clove, minced
1 Tbs. olive oil
4 14 oz. cans chicken broth
4 large baking potatoes, peeled and chopped
1 tsp. salt (if desired)
1/2 tsp. poultry seasoning
2 c. chopped deli-roasted chicken
1 5 oz. can evaporated milk
4 oz. uncooked egg noodles

Cook the first 4 ingredients in hot oil for 5 minutes, stirring constantly. Add chicken broth and the next 3 ingredients. Bring to boil; reduce heat, and simmer, partially covered, 25 minutes or until potatoes are tender. Add chicken, evaporated milk, and noodles; cook 10 minutes or until noodles are tender.

Hummus

Alexandra Hinich from The Great Family Cookbook Project

2 cans of garbanzo beans
2 tbsp tahini
2 cloves of garlic
1 oz of lemon juice
1 tsp salt
1 tsp of paprika (if desired)

Drain one can of the garbanzo beans and leave the liquid in the other. Combine all ingredients into food processor and blend until desired consistency is achieved. Can sprinkle top with paprika if desired.

Kamikazi Noodles

Andy Magner from The Zuelke Family Cookbook

12 ozs dry chow mein noodles
1 1/2 tsp sesame oil
1/3 c rice vinegar
juice and zest of one lime
1/2 cup soy sauce
2 tsp red pepper flakes
1/4 cup garlic chili sauce
2 tbsp sugar
2 cloves garlic, minced
1 cup grated carrots
3/4 c chopped fresh cilantro
3/4 c dry roasted peanuts chopped

Cook noodles as directed, drain, rinse and cool.

In large bowl combine oil, vinegar, lime juice and zest, soy sauce, red pepper flakes, garlic chili sauce, sugar and garlic. Mix until sugar is dissolved. Toss in carrots, peanuts and cilantro. Cut through noodles to manageable lengths. Toss with other ingredients. Chill for at least an hour. Add a little more soy sauce, vinegar or lime juice if dry. Can substitute fresh pasta. Sprinkle more chopped peanuts on top right before serving.

Loaded Baked Potato Soup

Aimee Zappa from Food for Friends

3 c broccoli florets, trimmed
3 med. baking potatoes, peeled and cubed
1 small onion, roughly chopped
1 (32 oz) carton reduced sodium chicken stock or broth
1 1/4 c. 2 % milk
1/4 c all purpose flour
1 (8-oz) block 2% sharp cheddar cheese, grated
salt and pepper to taste
toppings - extra cheese, sour cream, bacon bits, sliced green onions

Place broccoli, potatoes and onions in a large stockpot; cover with chicken stock. Bring to a boil; cover, reduce heat and simmer until veggies are tender (8-10 minutes). Using a wand or immersion blender, puree soup to desired texture (you can also transfer 1/2 at a time to a blender to puree). In a separate bowl, whisk together milk and flour. Pour into soup and return to heat, about 5 minutes (to cook the raw flour flavor out). Stir in grated cheese, reserving about 1/4 for topping. Stir constantly until cheese is completely melted. Serve topped with additional cheese, sour cream, bacon and green onions

Newfoundland Fish & Brewis

Rick Newman from Cooking Across The Generations: The Newman/ Poulin Family Cookbook

1 lb salt cod
4 hard biscuits [hard tack]
1/2 cup of salt pork cut into tiny cubes and fried [scrunchions]

Cut cod into serving-size pieces. Soak cod and hardbread separately in cold water for 8 hours or overnight. Change the cod water a couple of times.

Drain fish. In saucepan, cover fish with
cold water. Heat to boiling and boil gently for 15 to 20 minutes or until tender; drain. Meanwhile, in skillet, fry salt pork until golden and crunchy. Drain bread and place in saucepan, cover with salted water and bring to a full boil. Drain immediately and serve with fish on warm plates. Sprinkle with scrunchions.

Orzo Salad with Feta Cheese

Anne and Bill West from Roebken Family Cookbook

1 1/2 c. orzo
1/4 c. olive oil
Juice of one large lemon
1 tbsp. red wine vinegar
1/4 c. minced fresh parsley (I use more)
1/4 c. minced fresh dill (I use more)
1 1/2 c. cherry tomatoes halved
3/4 c. Greek olives
3/4 c. feta cheese crumbled
salt and pepper to taste

Soups, Stews, Salads and Sauces

Cook orzo in boiling water for 12 minutes or until just tender. Drain and place in serving bowl, stir in 1 tbsp. olive oil and cool to room temperature. Whisk juice, vinegar and remaining olive oil and mix into orzo. Gently mix in other ingredients. Serve at room temperature. (Sometimes I also add chopped fresh basil.)

Pasta Salad (Good Summer Salad)

Karen Malone from Recipes from Nannie Karen's Kitchen

2 cups small shells, cooked and cooled
1-2 chopped tomatoes
1 small grated onion
1\4 cup cucumber, chopped
1\2 cup green pepper, chopped
2\3 cup white sugar
1\2 cup canola oil or olive oil
1\3 cup ketchup
1\4 cup vinegar
salt & pepper

Mix all the ingredients together and refrigerate till ready to serve.

Potato Soup with Kale and Chorizo

Heather Fong from The Shogren Family Cookbook

5 tbsp olive oil, divided
2 cups onion, chopped
2 tsp smoked paprika
1-1/2 lbs. russet potatoes,
8 cups low-sodium chicken broth
1-1/2 lbs. kale
1 package garlic croutons
8 oz. fully cooked smoked Spanish chorizo or hot Calabrese salami, casing removed if necessary, chopped

Stem and tear kale into small pieces (about 16 cups lightly packed). Peel and cut potatoes into 1/4 inch slices. Heat 3 tbsp oil in large pot over medium heat. Add onion; cook until translucent, about 8 minutes. Add chorizo and paprika; stir 1 minute. Add potatoes and broth. Increase heat and bring to boil. Add kale; stir until wilted and soup returns to boil. Reduce heat to low, cover, and simmer 1 hour, stirring occasionally. DO AHEAD: Can be made 1 day ahead. Refrigerate uncovered until cool, then cover and chill. Warm before serving.

Red Bean Gumbo

Ryan Rojas from The Tasty Bourgeois Cookbook

2 27 oz cans of Blue Runner red beans
2 49 oz cans of Swanson's chicken broth
2 lbs. Andouille Sausage
½ lb. Tasso
1 cups of vegetable oil
1 cups of all purpose flour
2 medium Vidalia onions
1 medium red onion
1 green bell peppers
1 red bell pepper
1 bunch of parsley
1 bunch of Shallots
1 Tablespoons of minced garlic
Cooked rice

Cut-up all the veggies, keeping the greens of the shallots and the parsley separate. Take one can of the beans and blend them together with a little of the chicken stock (because it's easier to blend with a little more liquid) and tasso. You will have to cut the tasso in small manageable pieces for the blender to handle. In a heavy-bottomed large pot, add the flour and oil, then cook the roux over a low fire stirring the whole way until the roux is peanut butter in color. After the veggies are wilted, add the andouille and stir, after that has fried down for a couple of minutes, add the rest of the chicken stock, the blended red beans, the other can of beans(un blended) and the garlic....stir. If the gumbo looks too thick, you can add more water or more chicken stock, to achieve your desired consistency. (Keep your cover on if you have it perfect, cook with your cover off if you have to much liquid then add the cover later). Cook at a nice simmer and skim the grease as it comes to the top. Cook for at least an hour or hour and a half. Check if the gumbo is the right thickness(if it's too thin just take the cover off and boil off the excess liquid or add a little more water or chicken stock if it is too thick) add the parsley and green onion tops. Then you can do the seasoning(I normally use Tony Chachere's and salt) to taste...red pepper and salt works wonders too...depending on what you have. Serve over rice and enjoy

Reuben Soup

Mary Jo Creevy from Mary Jo's Family Cookbook Project

1 lb corned beef
½ c. sauerkraut
1 stick butter
½ c. flour
3 c. cream
2 c. milk
1 c. diced white onion (optional)
1-1/2 c. grated Swiss cheese
½ tsp. white pepper
¾ tsp. garlic salt
¾ tsp. onion powder
¾ tsp. celery salt
¾ tsp. lemon pepper
½ tsp. salt

Dice or shred corned beef. Combine corned beef w/sauerkraut and set aside.

Melt butter in large soup pot over low heat. Add flour and heat 3-5 minutes, stirring constantly to cook flour and make roux.

Stir in cream and milk. Add onions. Increase heat to medium and continue cooking 7-10 minutes; stirring constantly until soup thickens. Add cheese and stir to blend. Add white pepper, garlic salt, onion powder, celery salt, lemon pepper and salt. Add corned beef and sauerkraut. Stir until well-combined.

Salsa alla Rosa

Nonni Rose from The Anderson / Farinella Family Cookbook

1 lb. fresh spinach or swiss chard
1 lb. ricotta cheese
6 tbsp. milk or cream
1/2 tsp. nutmeg
1/2 cup butter
1/2 cup grated parmesan cheese
garlic powder to taste (optional)

Clean spinach or swiss chard. In a bowl combine the ricotta, milk, and nutmeg. In a large skillet melt the butter. Add the spinach or swiss chard and the ricotta mixture to the butter. Warm over low heat, do not cook. Stir in the grated cheese, and pour over hot pasta.

Seafood and Sausage Stew

Lynda Tolar from Cookbook Worthy

2 Pounds Raw Shrimp
1 Pound Crawfish Tails
7 Cups Water
4 Bay Leaves
3/4 Cup Light Roux
4 Tablespoons Butter
3 Cups Chopped Onions
2 Cups Chopped Bell Pepper
2 Cups Chopped Celery
1 1/2 Pounds Andouille Sausage Sliced
1 Pound Okra
3 Cloves Garlic, Minced
2 Teaspoons Salt
1 Teaspoon Black Pepper
1 Teaspoon Red Pepper
2 Cups Chopped Fresh Tomatoes
1 Pound Lumped Crab Meat
1 Onion Quartered
Hot Cooked Rice

Peel shrimp and crawfish, reserve shells; keep seafood in covered bowl in refrigerator. Put shells in stock pot with water, quartered onions and bay leaves. Bring to a boil, partly covered and simmer 20 minutes. Strain and set aside. Melt butter in large heavy sauce pan. Add onions, bell pepper and celery. Cook over medium heat until onions are soft. Approximately 6-8 minutes. Stir occasionally. Add sausage and mix well. Cook 5 minutes. Add okra and garlic; stir and cook unit okra stops producing white "threads"

Put 6 cups of stock back into stock pot and add remaining bay leaves, and salt, peppers (black and red). Bring to a boil, partly cover pan. Lower heat and simmer about 20 minutes. Stir in roux, mix well; simmer uncovered for 40 minutes, stirring occasionally. Stir in seafood and cook until shrimp turns pink. Serve over rice.

Spaghetti Sauce

Irene Snyder Houman from The Snyder/Johnson Family Cookbook Project

1 1/2 lbs ground beef
small chopped onion
1 clove minced garlic

1 can diced tomatoes
1 can tomato soup
1 small can V8
1/2 c catsup
1 large can mushrooms
1/8 cup parsley flakes
2 T oregano
2 bay leaves
salt and pepper to taste

Brown ground beef with onion and garlic. Add diced tomatoes, tomato soup, V8, catsup, mushrooms, oregano, parsley, salt and pepper and 2 bay leaves. Simmer about 1 hour or until thickened.

Spicy Pasta Faggioli

Cindy Rosarbo from La Famiglia Campano

2 cans Progresso cannellini beans
1 stick pepperoni cut into small pieces
2 cloves garlic minced
4 Tbsp. oil
1/2 can Hunts tomato sauce or
1 Tbsp. tomato paste
salt and pepper to taste
1/2 box cooked ditali or ditalini

In a medium sauce pan, sauté minced garlic in olive oil. Puree one can of beans including liquid and add to pan. Add the other can of whole beans and liquid. Add 2 cans of water. Add tomato sauce, pepperoni and salt and pepper. Cook down until thickened about 30 to 45 minutes. Cook and drain pasta leaving a little water and add to beans. Cook for a minute or two more and it's ready to serve.

Soups, Stews, Salads and Sauces

Summerfest Gazpacho

Lamar Yarbrough from Our Family Cookbook

2 lbs tomatoes
3 garlic cloves (crushed)
4 tsp olive oil
1 tsp salt
1/2 tsp ground cayenne
2 tsp lemon juice
1/4 cup red wine vinegar
2 celery stalks (diced)
1 large red onion (diced)
1 large cucumber (peeled, seeded, diced)
1 large green bell pepper (diced)
3 cups tomato juice
1/2 cup parsley (chopped)
1 cup water
2 tbsp worchestershire sauce
1 tsp celery seed
1/2 tsp tabasco.

Peel and dice tomatoes. Puree with garlic, olive oil, salt, cayenne, celery seed. Mix in remaining ingredients. Refrigerate overnight. Can be garnished with cantaloupe or honeydew melon and croutons.

Taco Soup

Gloria Cody from All My Children Gotta Eat

2 lbs. lean ground beef
2 cans pinto beans
2 cans chili beans
2 cans tomatoes with green chilies
2 cans hominy
2 c. chicken broth
1 pkg. ranch dressing mix
1 pkg. taco seasoning
1 medium onion, chopped
1 can diced green chilies

Brown ground beef in a large soup pan. Drain. Add all other ingredients. Simmer for about 1 hour.

Texas Style Chili

Lee Kleinman from The Kleinman Family Cookbook

1 lb. Ground Beef
1 lb. Beef Tips or Stew Meat
2 c Onion Chopped
2 T Garlic Chopped
2 Pablano Peppers (Seeded)
3 T Chili Powder
2 t Season Salt
1 t Black Pepper
10 oz can Tomatoes
1 c Water
Olive Oil
Flour

- 68 -

Cut Beef Tips into 1/2 inch pieces. Roast pablano peppers over gas burner or under broiler until skin bubbles and begins to turn black. Seed and chop roasted peppers. In a stock pot, saute onions, garlic and peppers in olive oil until onions are glassy. Remove from stock pot. In small batches, sear beef (Course, Chili Grind if available) in bottom of stock pot with olive oil. Use high heat and allow meat to caramelize and create a fond on bottom of the stock pot. Add beef, onions and peppers to the same stock pot. Add Tomatoes, water and seasonings. Simmer for 1-2 hours. Mix a few tablespoons of flour into some water and add as needed to thicken the chili.

Serve with grated cheese, fresh chopped onion and cornbread on the side.

Wellfleet Lobster Bisque

William Rice from The New Donovan Family Cookbook Volume II

3 slightly undercooked 1 1/2 lbs lobsters
6 T unsalted butter
1/2 cup brandy
1/2 cup + 3T shallots
3 cloves garlic, minced
2 tsp dried tarragon
2 whole bay leaves
1/2 tsp red pepper flakes
2 1/2 cups dry white wine
3 T tomato paste
5 cups water
3 1/2 T all-purpose flour
2 cups whole milk
1 cup heavy cream
sea salt and fresh ground pepper to taste
2 large egg yolks
3 T cream sherry

Remove meat from lobsters and reserve the shells. Dice the meat into 1/2 inch chunks and store, covered in the refrigerator until needed.

Melt 2 1/2 T butter over medium heat in a large skillet with sides at least 2" high. Add lobster shells (break if necessary) and toss until coated with butter. Pour in brandy and light with a long match. When flames die out, stir in 1/2 cup minced shallots, garlic, tarragon, bay leaves, and red pepper flakes. Mix in wine and tomato paste. Add water and let stock simmer for 45 minutes to an hour. Strain stock through a fine sieve into large bowl and discard solids.

Melt the remaining 3 1/2 T butter in a heavy soup pot over medium heat. Add remaining minced shallots and saute for 2 minutes until softened. Add flour and cook, whisking constantly, for 1 minute. Gradually whisk in the lobster stock slowly until thoroughly blended. Whisk in milk and heavy cream and cook over medium heat until hot. Season to taste with salt and pepper.

Whisk egg yolks together in another small bowl. Whisk in 1/2 cup of hot soup and then return mixture to the pot. whisk until blended. Do not let boil or it will curdle. Add lobster meat and sherry. Heat over low heat. Serve and enjoy.

Zesty Pork and Beans

Susan Privot from Family Recipes

4 slices bacon, cooked and diced
16 oz can pork and beans
1/4 c brown sugar
1/4 c chopped onion
1/2 tsp chopped garlic
1/4 c ketchup
1 tsp chili powder
1/2 tsp dry mustard

Preheat oven to 350º. Combine ingredients and bake 45 minutes or till hot and bubbly.

Main Courses: Beef, Pork and Lamb

Individual Pineapple Meat Loaves pg. 83

Oven Barbecued Pork Baby Back Ribs pg. 86

Red Jambalaya pg. 89

All-in-One Fiesta Stew Pot

Anne and Bill West from Roebken Family Cookbook

3 T flour
1 tsp. ground cumin
1/2 t chili powder
1/4 t ground cinnamon
2 tbsp. veg. oil
1 c. beef broth
1/2 c. apple juice
1 1/2 lb. lean beef chuck
6 small white potatoes
2 med. sweet potatoes
1 med. green bell pepper
1 medium red bell pepper
1 med. onion sliced thin
1 10 oz. can tomatoes with green chilies
1 8 oz. can tomato sauce
2 tbsp. honey
2 granny Smith apples
1 15oz. can kidney beans, drained
2 tbsp. parsley
Shredded cheddar cheese for garnish
Coarsely chopped black olives for garnish

Cut beef into 1 inch cubes. peeled and quarter potatoes. Core and seed peppers and then cut in 2 inch strips. Core and cut apples into 1 inch cubes. Combine flour, cumin, chili powder, garlic powder and cinnamon in a large bowl. Add the beef cubes and toss with a fork to coat. Brown beef in batches in oil in heavy pot. Return beef to the pot. Add broth and apple juice. Cover and simmer until meat is tender, about 1 hour.
Add potatoes, peppers, onion, tomatoes with chilies, tomato sauce and honey. Cover and simmer until potatoes are tender, about 30-35 minutes. Add apples and kidney beans, cover and simmer about 15 minutes. Stir in parsley and serve in shallow bowls . Garnish with cheese and olives.

Aunt Ceel's Lasagna!

DeeDee Duffy from The DiSalvatore Family Cookbook

2 lbs. Italian sausage
1 clove garlic, minced
1 T. basil
1 1/2 tsp. salt
1, 1 lb. can (2 cups) tomatoes
2, 6 oz. cans (1 1/3 cups) tomato paste
10 oz. lasagna noodles
1 1/2 cups ricotta cheese
1 1/2 cups creamy cottage cheese
1/2 c. grated Parmesan cheese
2 T. parsely flakes
2 beaten eggs
2 tsp. salt
1/2 tsp. pepper
1 lb. shredded Mozzarella cheese

Brown sausage slowly; spoon off excess fat. Add next 5 ingredients. Simmer uncovered 30 minutes, stirring occasionally. Cook noodles in large amount boiling salted water till tender; drain; rinse. Combine remaining ingredients, except Mozzarella cheese. Tip: before placing the noodles in a lasagna dish, my mom would use some of her sauce and spread a very thin layer over the bottom of the dish. That way the noodles on the bottom don't get hard. Place half the noodles in a lasagna dish; spread with half the cheese mixture, half Mozzarella and half the meat mixture. Repeat layers. Bake at 375ºF about 30 minutes. Let stand 10 minutes before cutting in squares - filling will set slightly. Makes 12 servings. *Or assemble early; refrigerate. Be sure to allow 15 minutes or so longer in the oven. Enjoy!

BBQ Pork Ribs

Eric Abramson from The Ward/Bagley/Blevins and Friends Family Cookbook

Country style pork boneless ribs
Your favorite BBQ sauce

Boil ribs in seasoned water for 20 minutes. Place ribs in a casserole dish with some of the water, about 2 inches. Cover tightly with foil. Bake at 250º for about 5 hours. The meat will be falling apart and your tummy will be going crazy, because it smells so good. Should have only about an inch of water left.
Add your favorite bbq sauce over the meat. Turn the oven up to 350º, place meat uncovered back in the oven for at least 10 minutes.

Beef and Broccoli

Karen Malone from Recipes from Nannie Karen's Kitchen

Fresh broccoli
1 lb beef (sirloin)
3 Tbsp. soy sauce
pepper
1 Tbsp. cornstarch
Drops of sesame oil
pinch garlic powder
4 Tbsp. peanut oil

Slice beef thinly across grain. Marinate with soy sauce, pepper, sesame oil and cornstarch for 15 minutes. Cut tops off of broccoli and cut the stalks diagonally into bite size pieces then steam broccoli with a little salt for 5 minutes (leave crunchy and put aside). In a wok or skillet, heat up oil. When hot, put in beef and garlic, stir fry until cooked. Add a little water and the broccoli to beef. Mix up and it is ready to serve.

Beef Carne Asada

Cathy Barbier Janet from Cathy's Favorites

2 round steaks (diced)
1 heaping tbsp flour
1 bell pepper, chopped
1 large onion, chopped
1/4 cup green onions, chopped
1 small can tomato sauce
1 small can mushrooms, drained
4 cloves garlic, minced
1 1/2 tbsp chopped peppercorns
salt and red pepper to taste
2-3 tbsp cumin
1 stalk celery, chopped
Flour tortillas

Small amt of olive oil to brown meat. Cook until juice is gone. Add and saute onions, bell pepper, celery, garlic. Stir in flour until pasty. Add tomato sauce. mix well. Add cumin, peppercorns and mushrooms. Add 1 1/2 cup water and simmer 1 1/2 hr or until meat is very tender. Cook until thick. Spoon into warmed flour tortilla, roll-up &

enjoy!

Beef Tips and Rice

Beth Medlin from Our Family Recipes

2 - 3 lbs sirloin tip roast
3 T flour
1 tsp salt
1/2 tsp pepper
2 tsp onion powder
2 cups beef bouillon
2 T cooking oil
1 pkg brown gravy mix

This works best in the crockpot. Cut roast into 1" cubes. Place flour, salt, pepper, meat tenderizer and onion powder in plastic bag. Add beef and coat well. In dutch oven, place oil and heat. Add meat and brown on all sides.Place meat, gravy mix and beef bouillon in crockpot and cook on low 6 - 8 hrs. Stir occasionally. Serve over cooked rice or noodles.

Beef Wellington for 2

Judie Jones from Buzzard's Best

2 6 oz Filet Mignon
1 tsp Dijon mustard
¼ tsp dried thyme
Salt and coarse ground pepper
1 Tbs butter
¼ cup goose liver pate or Duxelles
1 sheet puff pastry, 1/8 in thick
1 tsp milk
1 egg

Pre-heat oven to 425. Rub the fillet with mustard on all sides, then sprinkle salt, pepper and thyme on them. Melt butter in small skillet and sear fillet on all sides, about 5 minutes. Cool to room temperature. Place fillets on baking sheet and top with pate or duxelles. Cut out 2, 4-5 inch circles of pastry, you want it big enough to cover the fillet and touch the baking sheet. Drape the pastry on the fillet and pinch together at the bottom in 4-5 places to enclose the fillet. Trim off any edges that drape on the pan. Wisk the egg and milk together and brush on pastry. Decorate top with cut outs from pastry trimmings if desired.

Bake 15 minutes for Med Rare, serve immediately on a puddle of Creamed Mushroom sauce.

Duxelles is a mixture of finely chopped mushrooms, shallots and thyme, slowly cooked in butter until it is a thick paste.

Beef/Yorkshire Pudding

Marilee Larkey from Mom Loves to Cook

3 eggs
1 1/2 cups milk
1 t. salt
1 1/2 cups all purpose flour
1/2 cup butter or margarine
Combine first four ingredients. Beat until smooth and well blended. Melt butter in a 9 x 13 baking pan. Pour batter

into hot butter. Bake in preheated 425 degree oven 35-40 minutes, until brown and crusty. Cut into squares to serve. Serve with Beef Rouladen. Spoon pan juices over Yorkshire Pudding.

Brisket

Glenn Orndorff from Grammy's Family Cookbook

1 large brisket
garlic salt
1/2 c worchestershire sauce
1 tsp liquid smoke
1/2 tsp Tabasco sauce

Place brisket into a large cake pan or roaster pan, with the fat side up. Sprinkle with garlic salt, then pour the worchestershire sauce, liquid smoke and the Tabasco sauce over it. Cover pan with heavy duty foil. Place in the oven and bake all night at 200° - 225°. You may bake it for up to 12 hours at this temperature. This will make the most tender brisket. Cool brisket, and then slice. To serve, place brisket in a covered dish and reheat in a 350° oven for 30 minutes, or until hot.

Burrito Bundles

Barbara Mothershead from Mom's Favorite Recipes

2 lb hamburger
lg. bag shredded cheddar cheese
chopped green chilies
taco seasoning
refried beans
flour tortillas

Brown hamburger with taco seasoning. Drain well. Mix hamburger, cheese, green chilies, refried beans in a bowl. Place a large spoonful in center of each tortilla. Fold opposite sides to form a square. Heat and serve with salsa and sour cream.

Creamed Crock Pot Stew Meat

Tona Sauvageau from The Sauvageau Family Cookbook

4 lbs stew beef
2 cans 7-up
2 cans cream of mushroom soup
1 pkg onion soup mix

Combine above ingredients and put in crock pot. Cook on low 6-8 hours. Before serving, remove juice from crock pot and put into separate bowl. Thicken sauce with cornstarch and return to meat mixture. OPTIONAL BEFORE SERVING: you can also saute some fresh mushrooms and add to mixture. Serve over mashed potatoes or noodles.

Cuban Roast Pork

Annie Laurie Cisneros from Joy of the Repast: Favorite Recipes of Family and Friends

4 lbs. pork shoulder
2 tsp. cumin seeds
1/2 tsp. whole black peppercorns
4 cloves garlic, chopped
2 tsp. salt
1 tsp. dried oregano
1/3 cup orange juice
1/3 cup dry sherry
3 tbsp. lemon juice
3 tbsp. fresh lime juice
2 tbsp. olive oil

Trim and tie pork (or pork leg). Heat a small heavy skillet over medium heat. Add cumin seeds and peppercorns to the skillet; stir constantly until fragrant and beginning to brown, about 2 minutes. Cool. Using a mortar and pestle, crush toasted spices with garlic, salt, and oregano to make a paste. You can also do this in the small bowl of a food processor. Transfer to a small bowl, and stir in orange, lemon and lime juice, sherry, and olive oil. Place the pork in a large resealable plastic bag. Pour citrus marinade over meat, and seal. Refrigerate for 12 to 24 hours, turning the bag occasionally. Preheat over to 325 degrees. Transfer pork and marinade to roasting pan, and place in the oven. Roast for about 2 1/2 hours, (basting with pan juices frequently) or until an instant read thermometer inserted in the center reads 145 degrees. Add small amounts of water to the pan if it dries out. Transfer the pork to a carving board, cover loosely with foil and let rest for 15 minutes. Carve and serve.

Dad's Pan Seared Steaks

Alvin Martin from The Martin Family Cookbook

1 T. vegetable oil
coarse salt and cracked pepper
1 boneless rib-eye or New York strip steak, about 1 inch thick, room temperature

Preheat oven to 475. Preheat cast iron frying pan on stove with a little olive oil in the bottom on high heat, until it begins to smoke. Brush both sides of steak with olive oil. Salt and pepper steak on both sides. Sear steak in pan 3-4 minutes; until a dark crust has formed. Then put entire cast iron pan in preheated oven. Bake in hot oven for 5 to 7 minutes or as done as you would like it. Transfer to plate, let sit a few minutes. Slice across grain, serve with steak sauce.

Down Home Chopped BBQ

Cheryl Wright from Cooking with Family and Friends

2 Tsp red pepper flakes, crushed
2 tsp season salt
1 tsp black pepper, freshly ground
3/4 cup of apple cider vinegar
2 medium onion, finely chopped
1 T of granulate sugar.
2 cups of your favorite BBQ sauce
3 pounds pork shoulder roast, bone in or 2 1/2 pounds pork roast, boned & rolled

Rinse the pork roast and pat it dry with paper towels. Combine all the ingredients. Rub the mixture into all sides of the meat. Cover loosely with foil or wax paper and refrigerate overnight. Place the seasoned pork in a shallow roasting pan and let stand room temperature 1 hour. Pre-heat oven to 300F. Pour vinegar to taste over the pork. Add chopped onions. Roast the meat until done. Keep basting with the pan juice. Cook slow for about 5 hours.

Remove meat from the bone-chopped or pull the pork. add your favorite BBQ sauce.

Eric's Rosemary Flank Steak

Eric Ruderman from The Wiersch Family Cookbook

One flank steak (approx. 2 lbs)
½ cup soy sauce
½ cup olive oil
4 ½ T. honey
6 garlic cloves, minced
3 T. fresh rosemary
1 ½ T. black pepper
1 ½ tsp. salt

Marinade flank steak in a ziploc bag for 3 to 24 hours. Grill to desired temperature.

Florene Skaff's Loobi

Diane Marshall from The Schuldt Family Cookbook

1 lb. lamb, in 1 inch cubes
oil
1 (28 oz.) can whole tomatoes
1/2 c. tomato juice
1/2 med. onion, chopped
3/4 c. water
1 bay leaf
1/8 tsp. allspice
1/2 (1 lb.) bag green beans
salt
pepper

Add oil to medium large pot and brown meat (could use pork or beef). Salt and pepper meat as you brown it. Drain excess oil if needed. Add chopped onions and sauté until translucent. Drain juices from canned tomatoes: add drained juice, tomato juice, and water to pot. Add bay leaf, allspice, and more salt and pepper (I use lots of black pepper in this). Bring to a boil, cover, and simmer on low for 30 to 45 minutes until meat is tender. Add the tomatoes, coarsely chopped and the frozen green beans (could use Okra). Cook uncovered until beans are tender. Approximately, 10 to 15 minutes.

Serve over cooked white rice, rice pilaf, or couscous. Serves 3 to 4. Enjoy.

Frankie's Sausage and Pepper Spaghetti Pie

Frank Mattera from Francesco Mattera and Family Recipes

1 pound of linguine # 8
6 large eggs
Salt and pepper
6 ounces of grated cheese
2 large green peppers
6 sweet Italian sausage

In a large pot boil enough water to cook linguine as per package directions. Cut up both peppers and dice, then fry in olive oil, set aside. Cut up sausage into thin slices and cook until done, set aside. In a separate bowl beat 6 eggs and mix with a good amount of salt and pepper, add grated cheese and mix well, set aside.

After spaghetti is cooked, drain and place back in pot. Add in peppers and mix well, now add in cooked sausage, mix well, then add in egg mixture and mix well. Pour into 9" round 2 to 3 inch deep frying pan. Cover and cook on medium to low heat for about 8 minutes. Remove cover, lift and give a little shove. If mixture moves easily its time to turn. Place a large dish over frying pan and turn then slide mixture back into frying pan cover and cook another 8 minutes. Remove cover, place dish over frying pan, turn and remove. Serve warm and sliced like a pie.

French Dip Sandwiches

Jane Burke from Aelred and Rita Wagner Family Cookbook

1 package of onion soup
3 cups of boiling water
Beef roast
1 package of Good Seasons Dry Italian mix

This works great in a crock pot on slow cooking.
Mix the ingredients and pour over the roast and cook slowly until fork tender. Slice the meat and serve on a roll of your choice. Strain the broth and put into dipping bowls to increase the flavor and enjoyment of each bite.

Gluton Free Burgers

Sabreena Rabun from The Wellness Cookbook

1 lb. of ground beef or turkey
1/4 cup of gluten free ketchup
1/2 tbsp. chili powder
2 tsp. Worcestershire sauce
dash of ground red pepper
1/2 tsp. kosher salt

Combine everything together in a large bowl. Form into patties. Bake on 350 degrees F for about 20 minutes. Serve as you would a regular burger (gluton free bun or bread).

Main Courses: Beef, Pork and Lamb

Granny's Pork Chalupa

Glenna Crum from Favorite Recipes

4 lbs. pork loin roast
1 lb pinto beans
2 cloves garlic - chopped
2 tbsp. chili powder
1 tbsp. ground cumin
1 tsp. oregano
1 small can long green chilies - drained
1 tbsp. salt

Put all ingredients in a large pan and cover with water. Cook covered over low heat - adding water as needed. After 6 hours, take out bones and break up meat with fork. Uncover and cook 1 hour to thicken.

Serve over corn chips. Top with grated cheese, Shredded lettuce, diced tomatoes, olives, avocados and hot sauce.

Grilled Pork Loin with Jezebel Sauce

Carole Finger and Marie Banks - Teledyne Turbine Engines from The Toledo Area Chapter APA Celebrates National Payroll Week!

1 whole pork loin
12 oz. jar pineapple jam
10 oz. jar apple jelly
4 tsp. Dijon mustard
2 tsp. prepared Horseradish
Zesty Italian salad dressing

Marinade 1 whole pork loin in Zesty Italian salad dressing (all day in refrigerator). I put this in a large ziplock plastic bag; turn several times.

Make Jezebel Sauce by mixing Pineapple Jam, Apple Jelly, Dijon mustard and Horseradish and heat (on stove or in microwave).

Cook pork on the grill. Test with meat thermometer for doneness. Serve with warm Jezebel Sauce.

Ham Loaf

Verla Fuller from Memories of Love, Cooking and Great Smells!

1-1/2 lbs. lean pork, ground
1-1/2 lbs. ham, ground
2 eggs
1 cup bread crumbs
1 cup tomato sauce

Mix all together. Bake in a loaf pan set in water for 1-1/2 hours. Top with mustard sauce.

Individual Pineapple Meat Loaves

Allie Bourgeois from The Tasty Bourgeois Cookbook

1 beaten egg
1/2 cup quick-cooking rolled oats
1/2 cup finely chopped onion
1/4 cup finely chopped green pepper
1/4 teaspoon salt
1 pound lean ground beef
1 8-ounce can crushed pineapple (juice pack), drained
2 tablespoons bottled sweet-and-sour sauce

In a large mixing bowl stir together egg, oats, onion, green pepper, and salt. Add beef and pineapple; mix well.

Divide mixture into 6 equal portions. Shape each portion into a 4x2-inch loaf. Place loaves in a 13x9x2-inch pan.

Bake, uncovered, in a 350° oven for 30 to 35 minutes or till meat is no longer pink. Top each loaf with 1 teaspoon of the sweet-and-sour sauce, if desired.

Lamb Stew

Brenda Seals from A Double Portion

3 lbs organic lamb shoulder
3 tbs of fresh rosemary leaves
dash of cayenne pepper
1 Bay leaf
3 tablespoons of parsley
2 Tablespoons of roasted minced garlic
¾ cup of olive oil
2 pounds of organic new red potatoes
1 organic rutabaga
6 fresh organic carrots
1 cup of organic red onions chopped
½ cup of whole wheat flour
3 cans of organic free-range chicken broth
11/2 tsp soul seasoning
1 tablespoon roasted garlic

Cut lamb into bite size pieces. Heat ¼ cup olive oil in a skillet on medium high heat. Sprinkle lamb with flour and toss to coat. Add meat to heated oil and sear on all sides about 2 minutes on each side. Remove to a plate. Repeat with any remaining lamb. Add oil as needed. Place potatoes, carrots, and rutabaga in the pan used for the lamb. Season with salt and pepper and sauté until caramelized. Add residual whole wheat flour. Transfer potatoes, carrots, rutabaga and lamb to a Dutch oven. Add 3 cans of chicken broth, bay leaf, roasted garlic, rosemary, garlic pepper, soul seasoning and a dash of cayenne. Bring to a boil. Turn down and simmer for one hour.

Leg of Lamb

Lee English from The English Family Recipe Treasury

6 to 9 lb leg of lamb
1 clove garlic minced
1 small onion chopped
2 T olive oil
1/2 c lemon juice
2 T mint jelly
1 tsp salad herbs
5 T dark brown sugar
2 tsp salt
black pepper to taste

Saute' garlic & onion in oil. Add remaining ingredients & bring to a boil. Remove from heat. Place lamb in foil & pour sauce over it. Close it tightly & bake at 350 degrees 2 1/2 to 3 hours. Serve with additional mint jelly.

Marie's Spanish Rice

Diane Poulin Newman from Cooking Across The Generations: The Newman/ Poulin Family Cookbook

1-1/2 cups Minute Rice
4 tbsp butter
1/2 cup fresh garlic chopped
1 lb ground beef
1 large green pepper chopped
1 cup water
1 large can tomato paste
2 large cans diced tomatoes
1 large can tomato puree
1 tbsp onion powder
1 tbsp black pepper
1/2 cup yellow mustard
2 tbsp sugar
1 tbsp celery salt
1 tbsp garlic salt

Melt 2 tbsp butter in frying pan, add uncooked rice, heat over medium heat, stirring often until rice is brown. Remove from heat. In a large pot cook the garlic on low in 2 tbsp butter, stir often and cook for 3 minutes. Add the hamburg, break up meat into small pieces cook 4 minutes.

Add the green pepper, onion powder, pepper and celery salt, continue cooking until beef is browned.

Add the garlic salt and the canned tomatoes, the paste and the puree, mix thoroughly. Add the mustard, sugar and water and stir well. Add the browned rice and stir.

Cook on low to medium heat for at least 1-1/2 hours adding water to the middle of the pan and stirring frequently to keep mixture from sticking. Serve with garlic salt.

Marinated Leg of Lamb

Milly Noah from Grits to Gourmet

4 lb. boneless leg of lamb
1 large clove of garlic, minced
1 medium onion, chopped
2 T. olive oil
1/2 cup lemon juice
2 T. light brown sugar
2 T. mint jelly
2 tsp. salt
1 tsp. black pepper
3 tsp. herbs (thyme, tarragon, rosemary, marjoram)

Mix all ingredients except lamb in boiler and simmer 10 minutes. Prepare browning bag according to directions on box. Place leg of lamb in bag and pour marinade over it. Close tightly and marinate at least several hours or overnight, turning occasionally. Bake in preheated 350 degree oven 1 1/2 to 2 hours or until tender.

Mo Jo Marinated Pork Tenderloin

Michelle Rice from The New Donovan Family Cookbook Volume II

juice of 3 large oranges (1 1/2 c.)
juice of 2 large limes
6 T. olive oil
1/3 c. chopped fresh parsley
2 T. oregano
1 tsp. salt
2-12 to 14 oz. pork tenderloins

Pour 2/3 mojo marinade over tenderloins and store in ziploc bag overnight. Save remaining juice to pour over cooked meat. Grill pork until done. Let sit 10 minutes before cutting.

Mully's Pasties

Gerry Durkin from The Rogers' Girls Family Cookbook

3 c flour
1/2 to 1 tsp salt
1 1/4 c lard or shortening
3/4 c very cold water
5 or 6 medium red potatoes
3 medium or 2 large yellow onions
Parsley for flavor
butter (pat for each pasty)
salt and pepper (to taste)
2 lbs of meat--1/3 pound to each pasty (use loin tip, skirting or flank steak)

Measure flour and salt for pastry. Cut in lard until dough resembles small peas. Add water and divide into 6 equal parts.

Roll dough slightly oblong. Slice in layers on dough, first the potatoes, then the onions and last the meat, sliced or diced in thin strips. Bring pasty dough up from ends and crimp across the top. Making the pasty oblong eliminates the lump of dough on each end. Bake about 375° for 1 hour. Brush a little milk on top while baking.

Nanny Pat's Spaghetti

Patricia Thrasher-Waller from The Thrasher Family Cookbook Project

2 pounds ground round
2 pounds ground chuck
1 large onion, diced
1 large bell pepper diced
1 head of garlic, minced
3 Tablespoons dried parsley flakes
2 teaspoons dried oregano
2 teaspoons dried basil
2 teaspoons sugar
2 teaspoons salt
2 teaspoons course ground black pepper
4 14-ounce cans Hunt's diced tomatoes
2 12-ounce Hunts Tomato Paste
1 8-0z can Tomato Juice
3 cups water
3 pounds spaghetti

Brown meat in a large pan, add onion to sauté, add salt and black pepper. Place meat in a 6 quart crock pot. Place can tomatoes in a food processor and chop to fine tomato blend, add to meat. Add remaining sauce ingredients to crock pot. Blend well and cook on low for approximately 8 hours. If you desire to cook on the stove top, increase the water to 4 cups. Cook for approximately for 6-8 hours at low heat, stirring often.

Oven Barbecued Pork Baby Back Ribs

Dawn-Marie Sneed from Dawn-Marie's Favorite Family and Cookbook Recipes

5-6 lbs. pork back ribs
1/2 tsp. accent seasoning
2 T. packed brown sugar
1/4 tsp liquid smoke
2 c. fresh orange juice
1/4 tsp. minced garlic
2 T. fresh lemon juice
1/4 tsp black pepper
1 T. cornstarch

Combine all ingredients except ribs in medium saucepan. Stir over medium heat until mixture thickens. Place sections of ribs in roasting pan. Brush liberally with sauce. Cover with foil. Bake in 350° oven for 1 hour. Baste and cook for another 1/2 hour. Uncover during final 15 minutes of cooking to brown ribs slightly. Brush on additional sauce or dip ribs in sauce at serving time.

Overnight Barbecue Beef Sandwiches

Marsha Pickar from Memories

4-5 lb. boneless pork or beef roast
1/2 c. water
1 onion, sliced or chopped
1- 16 oz. bottle barbecue sauce
buns or French bread

Cook roast with water in crock pot on low heat 10 to 12 hours. Remove. Slice thin. Return to crock pot. Add onion & barbecue sauce. Cook on low for another 4-6 hours. Serve on buns or French bread.

Red Jambalaya

Harriet Duhe' Melancon from the kitchen of Gertrude Siears Duhe' from A Taste of Our Family

1 lb. Fresh Sausage
1 lb. Smoke Sausage
1 Pack Weiners
1 large onion chopped
4-6 cloves of garlic chopped
1 large bell pepper chopped
fresh chopped parsley
2 8 oz. cans tomato sauce
4 cups long grain rice
seasoning to taste
salt and fresh ground red pepper
4 cups of cold water

Rinse rice with cold water and leave to drain. In a large pot (Mamma always used a black iron pot) brown the fresh and smoked sausage, drain off some of the excess oil, add onions and bell peppers and saute on medium heat until onions are soft, add the weiners and the garlic at this time and saute for about 3 - 5 more minutes. Add the tomato sauce, parsley, rice, cold water (use the same cup to measure the water that you measured the rice with. You will want equal parts rice and water!) and seasoning.

Cook on medium heat uncoverd until the mixture comes to a slow rolling boil. When it comes to a boil cover, reduce heat to low and cook for 20 - 30 mins. Uncover, stir and check the rice for tenderness. If it is still not completely done cover and recheck in 5 mins.

Rich's Jambalaya

Richard Petty from The Cookbook of Our Favorite Foods and Memories

1 lb Polska Kielbasa or Andouille Sausage
2 or 3 Chicken Breasts
1 Onion, chopped
1 Red Pepper, chopped
2 Celery Stocks, chopped
1 clove of Garlic, chopped
28 oz Diced Tomatoes
1 T Cajun or Luzianna Seasoning
1 T Tabasco Sauce (or to taste)
1 T Worcestershire Sauce
1 T File Gumbo
1 1/2 C real rice

Cut the sausage into bite size chunks. Cut the chicken into bite size chunks. Use a large pot: Brown up the sausage. With a slotted spoon, remove the sausage from the pot, add the chicken, and cook the chicken in the sausage drippings. Add the sausage back in. Add vegetables. Add Cajun seasoning, Tabasco, and Worcestershire. Simmer for at least an hour. Add File Gumbo (it's a thickener, and it tweaks the taste). Simmer for 30 minutes. While simmering the last 30 minutes: Prepare the rice per the instructions on the box (1 1/2 cups of rice, 3 cups of water, cover, bring to boil, simmer 15 minutes, remove from heat, leave covered for another 5 minutes). Tip: To flavor the rice a bit, and add some heat, add a tablespoon of Tabasco to the water. Add rice to pot and stir it up. Serve.

Rustic Pork Ragu

Amy and Sarah Hollister from McKee Cooks

2 T. olive oil
1 2 ½-lb. boneless pork loin
2 t. kosher salt
1 t. freshly ground black pepper
1 lg. onion, chopped
2 sprigs fresh rosemary, leaves picked and chopped
4 cloves garlic, chopped
35 oz. crushed tomatoes with juices
1 lb. cooked pappardelle or other flat noodle
grated Romano cheese

Heat olive oil in Dutch oven over medium-high heat. Season pork with salt and pepper; sear on all sides until golden brown, 3-4 minutes per side. Remove pork; set aside. Add onion, rosemary and garlic; cook, stirring, until fragrant, 2 minutes. Add tomatoes and juices; stir with wooden spoon, scraping any bits of pork stuck to the bottom of the pot. Return pork to pot. Boil liquid, then reduce heat. Cover pot tightly; simmer on stovetop until pork is tender enough to fall apart, 2 ½-3 hours. Remove pork and, when cool enough to handle, shred into bite-size pieces. Add shredded pork back to stockpot. Simmer until hot. Serve over pasta with Romano sprinkled on top.

Stuffed Green Peppers

Tanya Goodman from Goodman Family and Friends Cookbook Favorites

4-5 green peppers
1 lb 93% lean ground beef
4 c of prepared minute rice
3 8oz cans of tomato sauce
3 tbsp sugar

Clean green peppers, cut off tops and clean seeds out of peppers. Place peppers in a deep baking pan. (Note: I use my non-stick stove top cookware that is oven safe) Brown ground beef and set aside. (Note: I only drain ground beef if there is a lot of fat). Make minute rice according to package. Mix rice and ground beef together and spoon into peppers. Any remaining mixture just pour over top peppers and around in pan. In a small bowl, mix tomato sauce and sugar, then pour over stuffed peppers. Cover with aluminum foil and bake at 350 for 1 hour or until peppers are fork tender. Serves 4. Preparation time is approximately 20 minutes.

Tasty Steak over Creamy Rice

Deborah Smith from The Warner Family and Friends' Cookbook

8 oz sliced mushrooms
1 c chopped onion
1 garlic clove, minced
2 tsp vegetable oil
1 lb sirloin in 1" cubes
1 1/2 c beef broth
2 T sherry
2 T tomato paste
1 tsp Worcestershire sauce
1/2 tsp pepper
3 c hot cooked rice
1/2 c lowfat sour cream
2 T chopped chives or parsley
1 T 1% milk
1 1/2 tsp horseradish

Saute mushrooms, onion and garlic in oil. Remove from skillet and set aside. Cook steak in same skillet until browned. Stir in vegetable mixture, broth, sherry, tomato paste, Worcestershire sauce and pepper. Add salt to taste. Simmer gently for 30 min. Combine rice with remaining ingredients: chives, sour cream, horseradish, and milk. Spoon steak mixture over rice and serve.

THE Best Meat Pie

Rick Newman from Cooking Across The Generations: The Newman/ Poulin Family Cookbook

2 pie crusts molded to fit a 9 inch cake pan.
1 stick butter
1 1/4 cup chopped onions
3/4 cup chopped celery
3/4 lb ground pork
3 tsp minced garlic
1 1/2 tsp dried thyme
2 tsp sweet paprika
2 tsp dried basil
3/4 lb ground beef
2 cups unpeeled red potatoes
2 cups beef stock
1/2 cup bread crumbs
4 8 oz packages low fat cream cheese
1 1/4 cup light cream
3 tbsp dried oregano
2 tsp dried thyme

Melt the butter in a large deep skillet over high heat. Add the onions and celery and cook about 3 minutes. Reduce heat to medium, add the pork, garlic and seasonings. Cook about four minutes breaking up the meat and stirring and scraping the pan, add the beef, mix thoroughly, lower the heat and simmer about 5 minutes.

Cut potatoes in quarters, place in processor and run a few seconds at a time until coarse. Add the potatoes, stock and bread crumbs to the meat, combine all ingredients and cook for about 10 minutes stirring frequently. Use strainer to drain the mixture, allow to sit in strainer for at least 15 minutes to drain and cool.

While cooling, make the topping by placing bread crumbs, softened cream cheese, cream, oregano and thyme in a large bowl. Beat with an electric mixer until blended.

Spoon the meat filling equally into the 2 pie crust covered cake pans. Carefully spread the topping equally over each pie, try not to mix it in with the filling. Bake at 350º for about 45 minutes.

The City Chicken Recipe

Jewell Dean Bundy Taylor from Cooking With The Cousins

1 lb. pork
1 lb. veal
oil or margarine
2 eggs, beaten
salt and pepper to taste
garlic powder to taste (optional)
1 c. bread crumbs
1 c. flour
1 Tbsp. baking powder
1 can cream of mushroom soup
milk
water
wooden skewers

Cut pork and veal into one-inch cubes. Thread pork and veal onto skewers; alternate, allowing 4 to 5 cubes per skewer. Beat eggs with salt, pepper, and garlic powder. Stir together bread crumbs, flour, and baking powder. Roll skewers of meat in egg mixture and then in bread crumb mixture. Sauté in oil over medium heat until brown, turning occasionally.

Place skewers in roasting pan. Stir together soup with one soup can of milk and one soup can of water. Pour over meat. Cover and bake in a 350 º oven for one hour, until tender. Uncover and bake 15 minutes longer.

Tourtière (Meat Pie)

Terri McCarthy from McCarthy Family Cookbook

1 lb. ground beef
3 lb. ground pork
2 or 3 onions, diced
2 c. mashed potatoes
2 c. bread crumbs
2 tsp. sage
1 tsp. salt
1/2 tsp. pepper

Place beef, pork and diced onions in a very large pot with enough water to cover level of meat. Cook and simmer for at least 30 minutes.

Add remaining ingredients and simmer until ready to place into pie crust. Once in crust and covered with crust, cook for 40 minutes at 350º F.

Other optional ingredients: Jimmy Dean Sausage with Sage will also work for ground pork. You can also replace mashed potatoes with potato flakes, and instead of bread crumbs use stale bread cut into cubes.

Tourtierre (Canadian Meat Pie)

Claire Huckins from Our family and friends cookbook project

2 lbs fresh ground pork
1 lb lean ground beef
2 1/2 lbs potatoes
2 medium onions chopped
2 tsp cinnamon
1/4 tsp ground nutmeg
1/4 tsp allspice
1/4 tsp ground cloves
1/8 tsp ground thyme
2 tsp salt
1/4 tsp pepper
2 unbaked pie crusts

Peel, cook and mash potatoes. Cook onions till clear in large pan, add ground meat. Cook slowly for 1 hour. stirring occasionally. Add mashed potatoes and spices. Mix well. Put filling between unbaked pie crusts while filling is still hot. Brush top crust with melted butter. Bake in 400° oven for 15 minutes and 375° oven until crust is golden (about an hour). Serve.

Personal Notes: Note: 10 serving size of instant mashed potatoes can be used instead of fresh white potatoes.

Pepperoni Chicken pg. 110

Main Courses:
Seafood, Poultry, Pasta and Casseroles

White Lasagna pg. 116

Tequila-Lime Shrimp pg. 115

Baja Fish Tacos

Bryan Donovan from The New Donovan Family Cookbook Volume II

1.5 lbs filet of tilapia
2-3 eggs
vegetable oil
Italian-style breadcrumbs
1 cabbage
sour cream
rice vinegar
lime
salsa
shredded Mexican cheese mix
tabasco
small corn tortillas

Cut filets into rough 1 in. x 1 in. pieces, dip each piece into raw beaten egg mix, place each piece into breadcrumbs and coat, fry in vegetable oil on medium-high heat.

Add sour cream (~1/2 cup) to 4 cups of finely shredded cabbage, mix well and slowly. Add rice vinegar to taste - cabbage should be coated lightly and it should taste tart.

Lightly brush corn tortillas with vegetable oil and saute until light brown, warm and slightly crispy - immediately fold to desired shape and let cool.

Place fried fish pieces in bottom of folded tortilla. Cover with shredded cheese then fill taco most of the way with cabbage - top with salsa, lime, and Tabasco.

Baked Chicken Reuben

Marilee Larkey from Mom Loves to Cook

4 boneless skinless chicken breasts
1/4 t. salt
1/8 t. pepper
4 slices Swiss cheese
1 1/4 cups Thousand Island Dressing
1 - 16 ounce can sauerkraut
1 T. chopped parsley.

Drain and press out excess liquid from sauerkraut. Place chicken in greased baking pan. Sprinkle with salt and pepper. Place sauerkraut over chicken; top with Swiss Cheese. Pour dressing evenly over cheese.

Cover with foil and bake in 325° oven for 1 1/2 hours or until a fork can be inserted in chicken with ease. Sprinkle with chopped parsley to serve.

Baked Creole Fish

Cathy Barbier Janet from Cathy's Favorites

1-3 lbs redfish or bass
1 stick margarine or butter
2 small cans tomato sauce
1 cup ketchup
1 tbsp lemon juice
1/2 cup onion, chopped
1/2 cup green onion, chopped
3 tbsp bell pepper, chopped
1 tbsp Lea & Perrin
1 tbsp Tabasco
1/2 cup brown sugar
2 gloves garlic, minced
salt and black pepper to taste
red pepper to taste

Place meat in baking dish. Bake at 350-degrees for 1 1/2 hours, covered. Serve with white rice.

Personal Notes: Also excellent with boneless chicken, shrimp or crawfish.

Best Ever Corn Casserole

Evelyn Bennett (Memere) from Bennett's & Beyond: A Family Cookbook

1 can whole kernel corn
1 can cream-style corn
1 (8oz) carton sour cream
1 egg
1 pkg. corn muffin mix (Jiffy)
1 small onion
salt, pepper, dried parsley to taste

Combine all ingredients and stir together; bake in a greased 8x8 inch casserole dish in 350° for 45 minutes.

Bobby's Chicken Parmesan

Melissa Wester from Nonna's Family & Friends Specialities

Chicken Breasts
Flour
Egg
Italian Bread Crumbs
Olive Oil
Mozzarella Cheese
Parmesan Cheese
Onion
Garlic
Hunk of Beef
Hunk of Pork
Tomato Paste (with Italian Herbs)
Tomato Puree
Parsley
Oregano
Basil
Baking Soda/ or Sugar
Chicken Breasts – pound until thin (can also use cutlets). Cut the pounded breast in half and coat the breasts in

flour (Shake in a plastic bag and then shake off excess). Dip breasts in an egg wash (add a little water to egg and whisk thoroughly). Coat chicken with Italian Bread Crumbs. Fry chicken in olive oil, until lightly browned. Put two (2) pieces together with a slice of mozzarella cheese.

Put a little sauce in the bottom of a pyrex dish and put the chicken on top. Put sauce on top of the chicken and sprinkle with parmesan cheese. Bake covered in a 350 oven until heated through.

Sauce:
Put some olive oil in a large pot, Add a thinly sliced onion and some chopped garlic. Saute til onion is translucent. Remove onion and garlic with a slotted spoon. Add a hunk of Beef and a hunk of Pork and brown on all sides.(Anything on sale, it is just for flavor!!) Remove meat. Add a can of tomato paste that has Italian herbs. Add 2-3 cans of tomato puree, a little at a time so the paste mixes in well. Add a little dried parsley, oregano and basil. Add the onions back in and the meat. Cook for at least two to three hours and stir often so the sauce does not stick to the pan. After about an hour, add a pinch of baking soda. (This takes some of the acid out of the tomatoes and makes the sauce sweeter. Do not add too much baking soda or you will have no taste to the sauce!!!!)

California Yum Yum

Aunt Bea from 'We Love You Alison' Cookbook

1 cup Sharp Cheddar Cheese
2 lbs. Ground Beef
1 large can Tomatoes
6 ounce can Tomato Paste
1 tsp. Salt
2 tbsp. Sugar
Pepper, and Garlic Powder to Taste
1 cup Sour Cream
12 ounce package Noodles
8 ounce Cream Cheese
6 Green Onions

Brown meat and drain. Add tomatoes, tomato paste and salt, sugar, pepper and garlic. Simmer 20 minutes. Cook noodles and drain.

Mix sour cream, cream cheese and chopped green onions. Add cooked noodles to this mixture. Place meat mixture in a 13x9x2-1/2" pan. Add noodle mixture on top of that. Cover with cheddar cheese. Cook at 350° for 1 hour or until bubbly. Can be prepared ahead of time and put in refrigerator or freezer.

Catalina Chicken

Lee English from The English Family Recipe Treasury

Chicken drumsticks or wings
8 oz bottle of catalina dressing
1 pkg dry onion soup mix
1 10 to 12 oz jar apricot or peach preserves

Mix ingredients together and heat to blend. Pour over chicken and bake at 350° for 1&1/2 hours or until done.

Cedar Plank Lime Ginger Salmon

Lamar Yarbrough from Our Family Cookbook

2 teaspoons grated fresh ginger
2 teaspoons soy sauce
1 teaspoon honey
4 thin slices fresh lime
Black pepper, fresh ground
2 fillets salmon, approx 6-8 oz each
1 large or 2 medium sized cedar planks, soaked

Top each salmon fillet with 1 tsp. ginger and drizzle with 1 tsp. soy sauce and 1/2 tsp. honey. Season with black pepper to taste and top each fillet with 2 lime slices. Place salmon in center of cedar plank(s). Planks should be presoaked in water a minimum of 30 minutes. Heat grill to approx 400°, then place plank on grill and cook for 6-8 minutes depending on thickness of fish. Fish should flake when done. There is no need to flip fish *.

* note... You can sear grill marks in fish if desired by carefully taking fillets off the cedar plank with a metal spatula and placing directly on hot grill for 10 - 15 seconds just before removing from grill.

Chicken and Broccoli Casserole

Grandma Bennett from Grandma Bennett's recipes

Several sprigs Broccoli
1 boned cooked chicken cut up
2 cans of cream chicken soup
1/4 cup cherry
3/4 or 1 cup mayonnaise
2 teas. curry powder
salt & pepper to taste

Layer broccoli or asparagus and chicken into 9x12 pan.
Mix together rest of the ingredient's. Pour over broccoli and chicken. Grate 1/2 lb sharp cheddar cheese and sprinkle over all. Bake 350° for 45 min to 1 hr.

Personal Notes: If you are planning to take this to a party double recipe and carry the recipe with you. It is best to make it (not bake) the day or two before and store in refrigerator. You can use Cream of Mushroom soup instead of Chicken.

Chicken Fricassee

Victoria Stroink from Oma Stroinks Recipes

½ c butter
2- 3 tbsp flour
3 c Chicken broth
Capers
Salt and pepper
1 egg yolk beaten
Nutmeg
1 Whole chicken 3-4 lbs
Leak
Celery
Carrot
Onion
Green pepper
Salt and pepper
Rice

Make a chicken soup by cooking whole chicken with water, celery, leak, carrot, onion and green pepper. Salt and Pepper. Takes approximately 40 minutes.

In a large pot melt butter and add flour to make a roue. Add salt and pepper to taste, add chicken broth enough to make a slightly thick sauce. Add capers to taste. Add cooked chicken pieces.

Serve over Rice.

Chicken Pot Pie

Kris Birkholz from The Cookbook of Our Favorite Foods and Memories

2 C Chicken, cooked and diced
1 can Cream of Potato Soup
1 can Cream of Celery Soup
1/3 C Milk
1/4 tsp Sage
1/4 tsp Pepper
1 pkg (2 crusts) refrigerated Pillsbury Pie Crusts
3 C frozen Veggie Mixture, thawed (Corn, Peas, Carrots and Green Bean mixture)

Lightly spray a pie plate with Pam. Place one pie crust in bottom. In a large bowl, combine remaining ingredients; spoon into pie crust. Place top crust on pie. Crimp edges and trim away excess dough. Using the tip of a knife, cut several slits in top crust. Place pie on a pizza pan to catch any spills. Bake at 375° for 45 to 50 minutes or until crust is golden brown.

Chicken Quesadillas

Kristin Konrad from Aelred and Rita Wagner Family Cookbook

2-1/2 cups shredded cooked chicken
2/3 cup salsa
1/3 cup green onions
3/4 teaspoon ground cumin
1/2 teaspoon salt
1/2 teaspoon dried oregano
6 flour tortillas (8 inch)
1/4 cup butter or margarine, melted
2 cup (8 ounces) shredded monterey jack cheese
(I use 1 cup cheddar and 1 cup monterey jack)
sour cream, extra salsa and guacamole

In a skillet, combine first 6 ingredients. Cook, uncovered, over medium heat for 10 minutes or until heated through, stirring occasionally. Brush one side of the tortillas with butter. Spoon 1/3 cup chicken mixture over half of the unbuttered side of each tortilla. Sprinkle with 1/3 cup cheese; fold plain side of tortilla over cheese. Place on a lightly greased baking sheet. Bake at 475° for 10 minutes or until crisp and golden brown. Cut into wedges; serve with sour cream, salsa and guacamole.

Chicken Spaghetti

Tona Sauvageau and Roger Rasmussen from The Sauvageau Family Cookbook

3 lbs of chicken
1 green pepper - chopped
1 onion - chopped
2 stalks of celery - diced
1 lb. Velveeta cheese - diced
2 cans Rotel Tomatoes with green chilies
1 stick butter
1 can Cream of Chicken soup
1 can Cream of Celery soup
1 lb. box of Angel Hair Pasta

Boil chicken with salt water till done and tear up - save broth - I use 1 can of chicken broth and 1 can of water to boil chicken in. Melt butter in saute pan and add green pepper, onion and celery.

Boil the angel hair pasta at same time till done and drain. Using a large 6 quart casserole, add everything you just sautéed in butter. Add the Velveeta cheese, rotel tomatoes and soups. Mix all together and then add cooked and drained pasta and some of the leftover broth from chicken --don't want to add too much and make it soupy, just enough to moisten the soups into a sauce. Cover and bake at 350º for 40 minutes.

Crawfish Étouffée

Lynda Tolar from Cookbook Worthy

6 Tablespoons Butter
1/4 Cup Flour
1 Cup Chopped Onions
1/2 Cup Chopped Green Bell Pepper
1/2 Cup Chopped Celery
1 Tablespoon Finely Minced Garlic
1 Pound Crawfish Tails
1 t Salt
1/4 t Fresh Ground Black Pepper
1/4 t Cayenne
1 t Fresh Lemon Juice
1/3 Cup Thinly Sliced Green Scallion Tops
1 T Finely Minced Fresh Parsley
1 Cup Cold Water

In a heavy 5 to 6 quart pot, melt the butter over low heat. Gradually add the flour, stirring constantly. Cook over low heat until a medium brown roux is formed (about 15 to 20 minutes). Quickly add the onion, green pepper, celery, and garlic and continue to cook, stirring frequently, until the vegetables are glazed and tender (about 20 minutes). Add the crawfish tails, salt, black pepper, cayenne, lemon juice, scallion tops, and parsley and mix well. Add the 1 cup cold water and bring to a boil, then lower the heat and simmer for 12 minutes, or until the crawfish tails are just tender, stirring frequently. Shortly before serving, heat the etoufee slowly over a low flame and gradually add 1 to 2 cups hot water to provide the gravy. Serve over rice.

Creamy Bowtie Chicken Pasta

Melinda Carreon from My Grandma's Kitchen

1 bag bowtie pasta
2 boneless,skinless chicken breasts
½ c sun dried tomatoes (prepared as directed on jar)
½ c green onions (chopped)
½ mushrooms (chopped)
1 tbsp olive oil
Crushed red pepper to taste
Garlic cream sauce (see recipe in the sauces section of this book)

Place olive oil in frying pan and heat on medium heat. Cut up chicken into small pieces and place in frying pan. Add red pepper to taste. When chicken is done add in sun dried tomatoes, onions and mushrooms and cook for a 3 minutes. You don't want to cook it too long or the vegetables will get soggy. Cook pasta as directed on package, you want the pasta al dente.

Prepare garlic cream sauce according to recipe in the sauces section of this book. Combine chicken mixture and pasta in a large bowl. Pour sauce over the top and mix well. Sprinkle additional Parmesan cheese on top to taste. Serve

Deep Dish Chicken Pot Pie

Maleah Snipes from The Snipes Family Cookbook Project

1 LB. Skinless, boneless chicken breast
1/4 Cup Italian Dressing
4 oz. Cream Cheese
2 T. flour
1/2 cup chicken broth
1 cup shredded cheese
1 pkg. frozen veggies or broccoli florets
1 refrigerated pie crust

For cheese you can use Cheddar, Swiss or Mozzarella. Cube chicken breast. Preheat oven to 375 °, Cook chicken in dressing in a large skillet 2 to 3 min, or until browned on both sides. Add cream cheese, cook and stir until melted. Add flour and mix well. Add broth and veggies, simmer 5 minutes. Right before you pour the mixture in the pie plate, mix in the shredded cheese. Pour mixture into a 10-inch deep dish pie plate. Arrange pie crust over filling; flute edges. Cut 4 slits in crust to allow steam to escape. Bake 30 min. or until crust is golden brown.

Egg and Bacon Spaghetti

Erika Manning from The Friends and Family Cookbook Project

8oz spaghetti noodles
1 lb bacon (cooked)
3 eggs
Parmesan cheese

Cook spagetti noodles like normal. Do not rinse noodles.
Cook bacon in large skillet (drain grease and leave in pan)
mix noodles in with bacon. Fry on medium to medium high heat. Crack 1 egg over noodles and stir in while cooking. Repeat with each egg. Mix until all eggs are cooked then remove from heat and serve with Parmesan cheese.

Finger Licken Hawaiian Chicken

Mollee Renee' Bundy from Home Sweet Home Recipes

frozen chicken tenders, thawed and cut into 2" pieces.
salt, pepper and onion salt
1 c. honey Dijon mustard
honey (optional)
Rice Chex© cereal, crushed
coconut flakes
instant potato flakes (optional)
2 Tbsp. cooking wine (optional)
1/4 c. pineapple juice
1 Tbsp. Worcestershire sauce
1/2 c. orange juice

Place chicken in a container (a large Ziploc© bag or plastic container). Mix cooking wine, pineapple juice, Worcestershire sauce and OJ for a marinade and pour over chicken. Toss the chicken to cover in marinade. Refrigerate for at least 4 hours.

Drain chicken. Discard marinade. Season with salt, pepper and onion salt to taste. (I omit the onion salt.) Dip chicken in mustard, (I add extra honey.) Roll chicken in a mixture of cereal, coconut, and potato flakes. Place on baking sheet sprayed with Pam. Bake at 350° for 15 minutes.

Fish with Lemon/Caper Sauce

Joe Ball from Cookin' with Balls II

White fish
Salt
Freshly ground black pepper
1/4 cup flour
2 tablespoons olive oil
1/4 cup minced shallots
2 tablespoons capers
2 lemons, juiced
1/2 cup dry white wine
2 stick butter, cut into cubes
1 tablespoon plus 1 teaspoon finely chopped fresh parsley leaves
2 cups assorted vegetables, blanched if needed (such as baby carrots, halved, thinly sliced squash, thinly sliced zucchini, thinly sliced shiitake mushrooms, thinly sliced red onions, etc,)

For fish - talapia is good, any fish that doesn't fall apart would work just fine 3 to 4 ounces per person. Season the fish with salt and pepper. Season the flour with salt and pepper. Dredge the fish in the flour, coating completely. In a large saute pan, over medium heat, add the oil. When the oil is hot, saute the fish for 2 to 3 minutes on each side. Remove the fish from the pan and set aside. Add the shallots and capers. Season with pepper. Saute for 1 minute. Add the lemon juice and wine. Bring the liquid to a boil. Reduce the heat to medium low and simmer until the liquid reduces by half, about 6 to 8 minutes. Whisk in the butter, a cube at a time. Season with salt and pepper. Stir in 1 tablespoon of parsley. Add the fish back into the sauce and simmer for 2 to 3 minutes. In another saute pan, heat the remaining tablespoon of the oil. When the oil is hot, add the vegetables. Season with salt and pepper. Saute for 2 to 3 minutes.

To serve, spoon the vegetables in the center of each plate. Place the fish on top of the vegetables and spoon the sauce over the fish. Garnish with remaining parsley.

Fried Rosemary Chicken

Kim Wolf Isaac from Eating with the Wolf Family

4 to 6 chicken breasts
2 eggs
flour
salt
pepper
sage
rosemary
enough olive oil to get about 1/2 an inch from the bottom of the frying pan.

I cut all of the "funky" stuff off of the chicken breasts and then I cut them into about 3 pieces each or you can cut them into strips. I then put them in a gallon baggie, close the bag and take out my frustrations of the day by beating the chicken with a meat tenderizing hammer (not sure what the technical name is for that). Then dredge all of the flattened out meat in the beaten egg mixture and then a flour mixture of salt, pepper, & sage (if you like sage). I then put the chicken in the hot oil and start cooking. After placing the chicken in the pan, I sprinkle rosemary over the top of the chicken and it flavors the oil and also sticks to the chicken. You don't want the temperature to be so hot that it burns easily. I cook on medium heat and turn them a few times and let them get a golden brown and then place on a couple of paper towels on a plate.

Glorified Spaghetti

Jean Thayer from Memories of Love, Cooking and Great Smells!

1 lb. lean ground sirloin
1 pkg. Jimmy Dean sage-flavored sausage
1 container sliced mushrooms
2 sm. cans sliced olives
1 lg. can diced tomatoes
2 lg. jars spaghetti sauce
6-8 garlic cloves, minced
2 Tbsp. oregano
1 onion, chopped
Freshly shredded Parmesan cheese
1 pkg. spaghetti
Olive oil

In a large pot, brown the meats in some olive oil. Add all remaining ingredients, including including juice from olives except cheese and spaghetti. Simmer for several hours. In another large pot, bring water to a boil and cook spaghetti. When done, drain water from spaghetti in a colander, return spaghetti to pot and add about 1/4 cup olive oil. Toss spaghetti to be sure it's thoroughly coated with oil. Combine spaghetti and sauce together in the larger of the two pots and mix thoroughly. Top with freshly shredded Parmesan. For sauce, I like Paul Newman's Sockaroonie.

Hamburger Casserole

Dorothy Martin from The Martin Family Cookbook

1 lb. ground beef
1/3 C chopped onion
1/3 tsp. chili powder
1/4 tsp. red pepper (just a quick dash)
1/2 tsp. salt
1 can tomato soup
1/3 C water
2 C cooked noodles
small can of whole kernel corn, drained

In skillet brown the beef and onion. Combine with seasonings, soup, water, corn, and drained noodles. Mix well. Put in 1 1/2 quart casserole dish in 350° oven for 30 minutes.

Healthy Alternative Seafood Gumbo

Brenda Seals from A Double Portion

1 pound package chicken andouille sausage, sliced
5 slices turkey ham, chopped into chunks
2 grilled chicken breast, cubed
3 slices of bacon, cooked
1 package of celery, sliced coarsely
1 red pepper, sliced coarsely
1 green pepper, sliced coarsely
1 yellow pepper, sliced coarsely
4 fresh tomatoes, quartered
1 onion
1/2 cup of flour
1/2 cup of olive or canola oil
2 teaspoons of gumbo file'
1 teaspoon of salt
1 teaspoon of pepper
1/2 teaspoon of tumeric
1/2 teaspoon crushed red pepper
4 cloves of garlic
1 tsp soul seasoning
32 ounces of organic chicken broth
1 salmon filet
1-2 pounds of shrimp
1 pound of Alaskan King Crab Legs

Add rendered bacon oil to canola oil to equal 1/2 cup and make a roux with flour and oil. Add chopped celery, onion, and pepper. Add tumeric and garlic. Add sausage and ham.

In a crockpot place tomatoes, chicken broth and seasoning excluding gumbo file'. Add ingredients from skillet. Add salmon filet and cook on high for 3 hours. Add chicken and gumbo file' Add shrimp and crab the last 5 minutes of cooking.

Italian Chicken

Karen Rankin from The Rankin Family Cookbook Project

2 large chicken breasts
2 beaten eggs
Italian bread crumbs
Oil to brown crumbs
2 cans sliced mushrooms
1 cup chicken broth
2 cups mozzarella
2 cups cheddar

Cut chicken into approximately 1" pieces, dip in egg wash then roll in bread crumbs. Brown on both sides in oil, Place in casserole. Top with mushrooms, cheeses and broth.
Bake at 325 degrees for 1 hour.

Mexican Chicken Casserole

Elizabeth Newmeyer from Herring Heritage Cookbook

4 skinless, boneless chicken breast halves
1 pkg. Spanish Rice
1 can Campbell's Cream of Chicken Soup
1 small can diced green chiles
1 can black beans
1 can corn or peas
1 1/3 C water
Salsa
Shredded Cheese
Tortilla chips (crushed)

Drain beans (pinto beans can be substituted) Spray a 12 x 8 baking dish with Pam. Dump in the package of rice (you can also use Lipton's Fiesta Sides Taco Rice) and seasonings. Add soup, water, corn, and beans. Mix together well. Top with chicken. Top chicken with salsa and crushed tortilla chips. Cover. Bake at 375 degrees for 45 minutes or until done. Top with cheese.

Monterey Jack Chicken

Beth Medlin from Our Family Recipes

5 cooked chicken breasts
1 can cream of chicken soup
3/4 cup milk
1 can chopped green chiles
1 small pkg corn tortillias
8 oz container sour cream
8 oz grated Monterey Jack Cheese w/Jalapenoes

Bake chicken and cut into bite size cubes. Cut tortillias into bite size pieces. Preheat oven to 350°. Mix together all ingredients except cheese. Turn into lightly buttered casserole dish. Bake 30-40 min. Sprinkle cheese on top of dish and return to oven until cheese melts.

Nancy's Seafood Fettucini

Nancy Alvord from Family Recipes To Remember

1-12oz. pkg. fettucini pasta
2 cups shrimp
2 cups crab
4 cloves garlic chopped
3 T. butter
1 cup chopped onion
2 cans chicken broth
3 cups half & half
1/4 tsp. nutmeg

Cook Pasta, set aside. In saute pan melt butter, add the onions and garlic, cook until soft, add seafood and chicken broth, cook 4 minutes on medium heat. Stir in the cream heat for 3 more minutes. Stir all of this into the pasta. Let cook for about 5-10 minutes until the pasta has absorbed some of the liquid, grate fresh nutmeg over top.

Nassau Grits

Milly Noah from Grits to Gourmet

6 slices bacon, cooked crisp
1 large onion
1 bell pepper
1 16 oz. can petite chopped tomatoes
2 cups chopped ham
1 cup grits, cook according to package directions

Saute onion and bell pepper in bacon drippings. Add tomatoes and cook until tender, about 20 minutes. Add crumbled bacon and ham. Add to cooked grits.

Oriental Chicken

Gloria Cody from All My Children Gotta Eat

1 can sliced pineapple
2 tbls. cornstarch
1 c. sugar
3/4 c. apple cider vinegar
1 tbls. soy sauce
1/4 tsp. ginger
1 chicken bouillon cube
1 large green pepper, sliced
1 chicken, cut up
1 c. flour
1/2 c. cooking oil
1 tsp. salt
1 tsp. pepper

For Sauce - Drain pineapple into a 2 c. measuring cup. Add water to make 1 1/2 cups. Mix in cornstarch to dissolve. In medium saucepan, combine sugar, syrup with cornstarch, vinegar, soy sauce, ginger, and bouillon cube. Bring to a boil and cook for 2 minutes.

Preheat oven to 400°. Coat chicken with flour. Heat oil in large frying pan. Brown chicken on all sides. Remove to a shallow baking pan. Sprinkle with salt and pepper. Add sauce. Bake uncovered for 30 minutes. Add pineapple slices and pepper slices. Bake for 30 more minutes. Serve with rice.

Paella

Brenda Neroni from A Fine Collection of Yum

1 Tbsp. of olive oil
salt and pepper to taste
3 lbs boneless chicken, cut into chunks
2 cups sliced chorizo, or smoked sausage
2 large yellow onions, diced
1 large green bell pepper, diced
1 large red bell pepper, diced
3 cloves of minced garlic
1 cup of Arborio, Valencia, or basmati rice
1/2 cup of dry white wine
1 pinch of saffron threads
2 Tbsp of paprika
3 cups of chicken stock
1 16 oz. can of diced tomatoes w/out liquid
1 bottle of clam broth
16 large shrimp,
16 little neck clams
16 mussels
1 large or 2 small lobster tail(s)
1 cup of fresh or frozen peas
1 cup of sliced Spanish olives (optional)
1 cup of artichokes (optional)
1 cup of diced roasted pepper or pimento

Split lobster in shells and cut in quarters. clean, shell, and de-vein shrimp. Heat olive oil in paella pan. Generously season chicken pieces with salt, pepper, and paprika. Brown the chicken on all sides and then remove from pan. Then sauté the chorizo or other smoked spicy sausage. Remove from pan. Sauté onion, garlic, and diced peppers until onions are translucent. Do not burn. Add rice, constantly stir and sauté the rice until it is light golden brown. Be careful not to over brown the rice. Then add 1 cup of the stock and saffron. Simmer until rice absorbs all the stock, stirring constantly. Add the chicken back to the pan and add wine, and remaining stock, 1/4 of a cup at a time. Stir until rice absorbs the liquids. Then add tomatoes and clam broth. Add additional stock or wine if necessary. Enough to rise 1/4 inch over rice. Add the chicken, shrimp, clams in shells, mussels, in shells and lobsters, quartered in shells, and push down into rice. Bake in oven for 8 to 10 minutes. Then add peas, artichokes, peppers, and olives which have been thinly sliced. Cover with foil loosely and bake an additional 5 minutes. Remove from oven and let sit for 5 minutes. Add more stock if dry or if you prefer it soupier! Do not overcook rice.

Penne in Cream Sauce with Sausage

Chip Lowell from In the Kitchen with Chip and Sally

1 tbsp butter
1 tbsp olive oil
1 medium onion, thinly sliced
3 garlic cloves, minced
1 lb sweet Italian sausage, casings removed
2/3 cup dry white wine
1 14 1/2 oz can diced peeled tomatoes with juices
1 cup whipping cream
6 tbsps chopped Italian parsley
1 lb penne pasta
1 cup freshly grated Parmesan cheese

Melt butter with oil in heavy large skillet over medium-high heat. Add onion and garlic and saute until golden brown and tender, about 7 minutes. Add sausage and saute until golden brown and cooked through, breaking up

Main Courses: Seafood, Poultry, Pasta and Casseroles

with back of spoon, about 7 minutes. Drain any excess drippings from skillet. Add wine to skillet and boil until almost all liquid evaporates, about 2 minutes. Add tomatoes with juices and simmer 3 minutes. Add cream and simmer until sauce thickens slightly, about 5 minutes. Stir in 4 tablespoons parsley. Season to taste with salt and pepper. Remove from heat. (Sauce can be prepared 1 day ahead. Cover and refrigerate.)

Cook pasta in large pot of boiling salted water until tender but still firm to bite. Drain pasta; transfer to large bowl.

Bring sauce to simmer. Pour sauce over pasta. Add 3/4 cup cheese and toss to coat. Sprinkle with remaining 1/4 cup cheese and 2 tablespoons parsley.

Personal Notes: Sandy "Schoolteacher" Smith made this for us 2/12/09 for me helping with her PC.

Pepperoni Chicken

Allie Bourgeois from The Tasty Bourgeois Cookbook

4 large boneless, skinless chicken breasts
4 ounces pepperoni, sliced
3/4 cup provolone cheese, grated
3/4 cup mozzarella, grated
2 cups Italian seasoned breadcrumbs
1 1/2 cups marinara
1/4 cup grated Parmesan cheese
Spray oil

Place each chicken breast between plastic wrap and lightly beat with a meat mallet until fairly thin.
Mix the provolone and mozzarella. Place a breast (smooth side down) on a cutting board. Place 1/4 of the pepperoni on the chicken in a thin layer. Place 1/4 of the cheese mix in the center of the chicken. Bring the sides in slightly and roll up (like an egg roll).
Spray a medium casserole dish with the oil. Roll the chicken in the breadcrumbs and place in the dish, seam side down. Spray the chicken with a little oil. Bake at 375 degrees F for about 25 minutes or until lightly brown. Top with warm sauce and garnish with Parmesan. You can use your favorite tomato sauce for pasta in place of marinara if you wish.

Pizza Rustica

Nonni Rose from The Anderson / Farinella Family Cookbook

14 cups flour
4 tbsp. active dry yeast
5 cups warm water (about 110 degrees)
1 egg (optional)
a stick of butter or olive oil (optional)
4 large ricottas
2 semi hard fresh cheese (cubed)
1 lb. mozzarella (cubed)
1 lb. provolone (cubed)
12 eggs
3 or 5 lb. canned ham

Remove ham from can, wash and put it on a dish with paper towels in the fridge a day ahead. Then cut it into cubes.

Mix together flour, yeast, water, egg and butter for your dough and let it rise until doubled, about 1 hour.

Mix together all of the filling ingredients. When dough is ready cut sizes for 1 extra large pan or 2 medium pans. Lay dough on bottom of pan, add the filling, and place another piece of dough on top. Seal the edges, and brush with beaten egg. Bake at 350 degrees for about 3 hours depending on the size of the pan, or until tested with a knife in the center and it comes out dry.

Salmon Loaf

Marian Bagley from The Ward/Bagley/Blevins and Friends Family Cookbook

1/2 cup cracker crumbs
1 can salmon
2/3 cup thick white sauce
2 eggs separated
1 tsp chopped parsley

Separate 2 eggs. Beat yolks and stiffen whites. Make white sauce and let cool. Add ingredients. Bake at 300° for 40 minutes.

Sausage, Shrimp and Zucchini Casserole

Steve Campano from La Famiglia Campano

2 medium onions finely chopped
2 leeks
4 cups of shredded zucchini
1 lb chorizo or andouille sausage
1 lb medium shrimp peeled
2 cups of shredded Italian cheese blend (mozzarella and parmesan)
½ cup bread crumbs
1 tbsp minced garlic
1 tsp Fresh oregano, finely chopped
1 tsp Italian seasoning
Ground black pepper
Salt
1 tsp Zararain's cajun seasoning
3 eggs
Pillsbury crescent roll dough

Quarter and cut leeks into about 1 ½ inch pieces. Split sausage in half and cut into bite sized pieces. In a large, heavy bottomed pot or dutch oven, fry up the sausage in a little olive oil. Drain excess grease and moisture. Add chopped onions and cook until tender. Add leeks and garlic and cook covered until leeks wilt, stirring occasionally. Add zucchini, about 1 tsp Italian seasoning, salt and pepper and cook until zucchini wilts and most of the moisture cooks off, about 8-10 minutes. Season shrimp with Zatarains and add to pot with about 1 tsp of chopped, fresh oregano and cook until pink. Remove from heat and let cool for about 15 minutes.

Add enough breadcrumbs to cooled mixture to absorb excess moisture. Crack eggs into the mixture and stir well to combine. Add cheese and mix well. Adjust seasoning to taste with additional Zatarains and Italian seasoning. Pour into a greased 9"x11" baking dish and cover evenly with crescent roll triangles. Sprinkle parmesan cheese over the top and bake in 375° oven for about 20 minutes, until crust is golden brown. Let it sit for about 10 minutes before serving.

Scalloped Oysters

Ann L. Richardson from The Richardson Family Cookbook

3 eggs, beaten
2 small cans Cove oysters
1 14 oz. can sweetened condensed milk
1 can (scant) milk
1 sleeve saltine crackers, crushed
1 1/2 sticks butter, divided

Preheat oven to 375°. Put eggs in a bowl and beat well. Add oysters with juice. Add the milks. Add crushed crackers. Melt 1 stick butter and add to mixture. Pour into 9"x9"x2" pan. Cut up remaining 1/2 stick butter in small pieces and scatter over the top. Reduce heat to 350° and bake for 35 to 45 min. until puffed and browned and center is set.

Shrimp Gumbo

Edith Warner from The Warner Family and Friends' Cookbook

1 lb. fresh shrimp
4 tbsp. bacon fat
4-5 onions -coarsely cut
4-5 green peppers - coarsely cut
1 10 oz. pkg. frozen okra
1 large can crushed tomatoes
6-7 bay leaves
1 tsp. thyme
1/2 tsp. salt
1/4 tsp. pepper
7 cups hot cooked rice

Peel and devein shrimp and set aside. Heat bacon fat in large fry pan. Add onions and peppers. Saute 5 min. Don't brown. Add tomatoes, bay leaves, thyme, salt and pepper. Cover and simmer about 1 hour. Then add okra. After 20 min. add shrimp and simmer about 10 min. until shrimp are pink and done. Be sure to remove bay leaves! Serve over hot rice.
Note: Okra also comes in 16 oz. bags. Use about 10 oz.

Smokin Macaroni & Cheese

Shanna Lasley from The Lasley's Favorite Cookbook

1 lb. cellentani pasta
2 tbsp. butter
3 tbsp. flour
1 (12oz.) can evaporated milk
2 cups shredded smoked gouda
1 pkg. cream cheese, softened
3/4 tsp. salt
1/2 tsp. ground red pepper, divided
8 oz. pkg. chopped cooked smoked ham
2 cups cornflakes, crushed
2 tbsp. butter melted

Preheat oven to 350°. Prepare pasta. Transfer hot pasta to large bowl. Melt 2 tbsp. butter in med. saucepan over med heat; gradually whisk in flour until smooth; cook whisking constantly 1 min. Gradually whisk in milk and evap milk; cook whisking constantly 3-5 min. or until thickened. Whisk in gouda, cream cheese, salt and 1/4 tsp. red pepper until smooth. Remove from heat stir in ham. Combine pasta and pour into lightly greased 13x9 baking dish. Stir together cereal and 2 tbsp. melted butter. Sprinkle over pasta and bake for 30 minutes or until golden and bubbly.

Spicy Catfish with Sweet Potatos

Carolyn Collins from Southern Family Cookbook Project

4 catfish filets
2 medium sweet potatoes diced
1 medium red onion diced
4 T. olive oil
2 big pats butter
1 lime (a real one)
2 Hass avocados diced
juice of 1/2 lemon
2 Roma tomatoes diced
1/4 bunch cilantro roughly chopped
1 green onion finely chopped
1/4 tsp. salt
1 tsp. black pepper (fresh ground is better)
1 T. Tony's seasoning

Season catfish with Tony's on both sides. set aside.
Seed avocados (save seed and root it to grow an avocado tree) dice in small chunks and toss with the lemon juice to keep from browning, set in fridge.

Put 2 T. olive oil and one pat of butter in saute skillet on medium, add diced sweet potatoes and red onions, cover to capture steam to help the tenderizing process for the first couple of minutes, uncover and stir, continue to saute until tender. Empty contents to a big pretty serving plate.

Using same saute skillet add remaining 2 T. olive oil and butter pat...heat to medium and put in seasoned catfish fillets. cook about 4 to 6 minutes on each side depending on how thick they are until done. Lay each fillet next to one another over potato and onion mixture.
Mix Roma tomato, cilantro, green onion and avocado, salt and pepper...mix together. I do all this with my hands on the counter but you can use a bowl. try not to break up the avocado chunks. Put this over the top of the catfish. Yuuuummmm. So fresh...makes you feel you are really eating healthy.

Stuffed Chicken Breasts with Prosciutto, Dried Tomato and Artichokes
DeeDee Duffy from The DiSalvatore Family Cookbook

Chicken breasts, boneless
Prosciutto
Sun-dried tomatoes in olive oil
Artichoke hearts in olive oil
Romano or Parmesan cheese
Salt and pepper
Fresh garlic, minced
Paprika
Kitchen string
Olive oil

Preheat oven to 350°F. Pound with a mallet to flatten the chicken breasts to about a half-inch thickness. The thinner the breast, the easier it will be to roll the chicken around the other ingredients. If the breasts are thick, you can filet them by cutting lengthwise and then flatten some more. Drain the tomatoes and drain the artichoke hearts. Season the chicken with salt and a dash of pepper, go easy on the pepper. Layer the chicken with a little bit of minced garlic, then the cheese, then the prosciutto, then one or more sun-dried tomatoes, then one or more artichoke hearts. At this point look at the chicken with ingredients and guesstimate how long a piece of string you will need and cut to size. It's better to have a longer piece, you can trim the extra off later. Cut as many pieces of string as pieces of chicken. Roll the chicken; if some of the inside pokes out of the ends of the chicken, that's okay. Tie the string around the chicken tightly so it doesn't fall apart while searing. In a saucepan, heat olive oil; sear and brown the chicken on all sides. Transfer the browned chicken to a large roasting pan or glass lasagna dish with some space in between each rolled breast. Drizzle a little bit of olive oil over the stuffed chicken. Sprinkle with paprika. Bake at 350°F until done. Check after 20 minutes, if browning too quickly cover until done. Before serving, remove string and sprinkle with fresh parsley or cilantro.

Stuffed Chicken Rolls

Fred Mattera from Francesco Mattera and Family Recipes

6 boneless skinless chick breasts
1 cup water
2 eggs
1 package stuffing mix
1 can cream of chicken soup
1/2 cup milk
1 tsp. paprika

Make stuffing mix and add 1 cup water. Let stand on side 5 minutes. Add eggs: Spread stuffing on chicken breasts stay away from edges of chicken. Roll breasts short side to thicker side. Place chicken rolls seams down In 13x9-inch. Mix soup mix and milk. Pour over chicken. Sprinkle w/paprika. Bake at 400 for 30 minutes.

Tater Tot Casserole

Marcy Curran from The Rogers' Girls Family Cookbook

1 1/2 lbs. Hamburger
1 medium Onion, chopped
2 lb. pkg. Tater Tots
2 cans Cream of Chicken Soup
3/4 soup can of milk
Cheddar cheese

Cook hamburger and onion. Pour into a 9 x 13 inch pan. Layer the tater tots on top of onions and hamburger. Add cheddar cheese over tater tots. Mix the soup with milk until smooth and pour over. Bake uncovered for 1 hour at 350°.

Tequila-Lime Shrimp
Anneta Sudlow - Cooper Tire & Rubber Company from The Toledo Area Chapter APA Celebrates National Payroll Week!

1/3 cup fresh lime juice
1/2 Tbsp jalapeño pepper(s), minced
1/2 tsp chili powder, chipotle-variety
3/4 tsp sugar
3/4 fl oz tequila
1/4 cup fresh cilantro
1 Tbsp olive oil
1 medium minced garlic clove(s)
1/2 tsp sea salt, or to taste
1 1/2 pound shrimp, jumbo-size, shelled and deveined (or leave tails on for a nicer presentation)

Chop and divide cilantro. In a small bowl, combine lime juice, jalapeño, chili powder, sugar, tequila and 2 tablespoon of cilantro; set aside. Heat oil in a large nonstick skillet over medium heat. Add garlic and salt; cook, stirring, until garlic is fragrant, about 1 minute. Add shrimp; sauté, until shrimp turn pink, about 4 minutes. Remove shrimp to a serving plate and cover to keep warm. Add lime juice mixture to same skillet and place over high heat. Cook until alcohol burns off, stirring and scrapping sides of pan, about 2 minutes; pour over shrimp and garnish with remaining cilantro and more sea salt, if desired. Yields about 3 ounces of shrimp per serving.

Tuna Salad Bake
Doris Parkins from Parkins Family Cookbook

1 can cream of chicken soup
1 c. diced celery
1/4 c. finely chopped onion
1/2 c. mayonnaise or salad dressing
dash pepper
3 hard cooked eggs, sliced
1 - 6 1/2, 7 or 9 1/4 oz. can tuna, well drained
2 cups broken potato chips

Combine first 5 ingredients, fold in egg slices & tuna. Put into a 10 x 6 x 1 1/2 in. baking dish. Top with potato chips. Bake at 400° for 30 mins.

Whitcher's Gararge Tuna Tune-up Casserole
Karon Davenport Nason 1954 from The Whitcher Family Descendants Cookbook

1 Package medium noodles - 2 cups
2 medium onion - chopped fine
2 Tbsp butter of margarine
1 - 20 ounce can tomatoes
1/4 teaspoon garlic salt
1 teaspoon salt
1/4 teaspoon pepper
1/4 cup snipped parsley
1 7-ounce can solid white tuna
1/2 pound American Cheese slices

About 1 hour before dinner, cook noodles according to package directions, adding the chopped onions. Drain, Add butter.

In a bowl combine the tomatoes, garlic salt, salt, pepper and parsley. In an 8 inch square baking dish place half the noodles, half tuna, half cheese and pour half of the tomato mixture over the layers. Repeat layers ending with tomato mixture. Bake covered @ 350 degree oven - 45 minutes.

White Lasagna

Julie Soderberg Kyle from Lewis Girl's Lucky Duck Cookbook

1 1/2 lbs. ground pork sausage or beef
1 c. chopped onion
1/2 c. chopped celery
2 garlic cloves, minced
2 tsp. dried basil
1 tsp. dried oregano
1/2 tsp. dried Italian seasoning
1/2 tsp. salt
1 c. half and half
1 (3 oz.) package cream cheese
1/2 c. white cooking wine
2 c. (8 oz.) shredded Cheddar cheese
1 1/2 c. (6 oz.) shredded Gouda cheese
1 (12 oz.) container cottage cheese
1 large egg
8 lasagna noodles, cooked
2 cups (8 oz.) shredded mozzarella cheese

Cook first 4 ingredients in a skillet over medium heat, stirring until sausage is crumbled and no longer pink. Stir in basil and next 5 ingredients. Stir in wine, Cheddar and Gouda cheese; cook, stirring constantly until cheese is melted. Set aside. Combine cottage cheese and egg. Spray pan with PAM; spread bottom with a little bit of sauce. Arrange one third of noodles; layer with one third of meat mixture, 1/3 of cottage cheese and 1/3 of mozzarella. Repeat layers. Bake at 350° for 40 minutes. Let stand at room temperature for 10 minutes before serving.

Wild Rice Crab Cakes

Janet Zuelke from The Zuelke Family Cookbook

1 1/2 C water
1/2 C uncooked wild rice
1 pound Dungeness crab meat (drained)
3/4 C dry bread crumbs
1/2 C finely chopped red bell pepper
1/4 C minced shallots
1/4 C light mayo
2 Tblsp Dijon mustard 1 1/2 Tblsp lemon juice
1/2 tsp salt
1/2 tsp ground cumin
1/8 tsp ground red pepper
1/8 tsp black pepper
2 large egg whites(beaten lightly)
4 tsps olive oil (divided)

Bring water to boil in a medium saucepan. Add wild rice, cover,reduce heat and simmer one hour or until tender. Combine cooked rice, crab, and next 11 ingredients (bread crumbs through egg whites) in a large bowl. Divide the mixture into 8 equal portions shaping each into a 1 inch thich patty. Heat 2 tsps oil in a large heavy skillet over medium heat. Add 4 of the patties and cook for 4 minutes on each side or until toasty brown. Turn only once. Repeat with remaining oil and the other 4 patties. Serve with favorite tartar or aoli sauce or good mustard.

Williamsburg Chicken

Kelly Sankovich from The Schuldt Family Cookbook

9 - 12 skinless, boneless chicken breasts
7 oz. Swiss cheese, sliced
1 family size can cream of chicken soup
1 half a soup can milk
8 oz. herb stuffing, crushed
3/4 stick butter

Place chicken in a greased 9 x 13 inch pan. Layer Swiss cheese over chicken. Mix soup and milk and pour over cheese. Melt butter and combine with crushed stuffing. Sprinkle stuffing over all. Can be refrigerated overnight. Cover with foil and bake at 350° for 1 hour. Uncover and bake another 1/2 hour. Leftovers freeze well.

Vegetables and Vegetarian Dishes

Roasted Potatoes with Artichokes & Feta pg. 131

Judy's Chili Rellenos pg. 128

Spicy Shrimp Stuffed Mirliton pg. 132

Artichoke Bake

Brenda Neroni from A Fine Collection of Yum

16 to 20 ounces frozen artichoke hearts
1/4 cup butter
3/4 teaspoon salt
cracked pepper
1 teaspoon onion powder
1/4 teaspoon dry mustard
1/3 cup all-purpose flour
1 1/2 cups milk
1 egg, lightly beaten
1/2 cup grated mild cheddar cheese
1 tablespoon fine dry bread crumbs
paprika, optional

Cook artichokes as directed on package. Drain and reserve 1/2 cup of the liquid. Melt butter in a saucepan over low heat; stir in flour, salt, pepper, onion powder, and dry mustard. When flour mixture is smooth and bubbly, gradually stir in reserved cooking liquid and milk. Cook over low heat, stirring constantly, until thickened. Remove from heat. Combine beaten egg with half of grated cheese. Gradually stir hot sauce mixture into egg and cheese mixture. Blend well. Place artichokes in a shallow baking dish in a single layer. Pour sauce over artichokes; sprinkle with cheese, bread crumbs, and sprinkle with paprika if using. Bake at 425° for 18 to 22 minutes.

Artichoke dip

Susan Privot from Family Recipes

8 oz cream cheese
4 tbsp mayonnaise
8 oz jar artichokes, drained
½ c parmesan cheese
4 oz can mild chiles
4 oz grated cheddar cheese
Big corn chips

Into a food processor put cream cheese and mayonnaise. Pulse till smooth. Add artichokes, parmesan and mild chilies. Pulse till coarsely chopped, but fully incorporated together. Put in a baking dish; top with cheddar cheese. Bake at 375 degrees for 20-30 minutes or till hot and bubbly.

Serve with big corn chips.

Au Gratin Potatoes Made Cheesy & Easy

Whitney J. Bundy from Home Sweet Home Recipes

6 - 8 medium-sized potatoes
salt and pepper to taste
1 medium onion, chopped (divided)
1 can cream of mushroom soup (divided)
2 c. shredded cheddar cheese (divided)

Boil potatoes in their jackets. Thinly slice potatoes when cool.

Spray 3-quart casserole dish with cooking spray. Place layer of potato slices in bottom of casserole dish. Salt and pepper potatoes to taste. Sprinkle layer of onions over potatoes. Pour part of the can of cream of mushroom soup over onions and potatoes. Sprinkle with shredded cheddar cheese. Repeat layers (potatoes, salt and pepper, onions, soup and cheese) ending with cheese on top.

Bake in 350° oven for 30-40 minutes or until onions rise to the top.

Back Fire Beans

Kelvin Bundy from Cooking With The Cousins

1 can butter beans, drained
1 can kidney beans, drained
1 can baked beans
1 lb. bacon, cooked and chopped
1 can pork and beans
1 c. cheddar cheese
1/4 c. Parmesan cheese
1/2 c. brown sugar
1/3 c. ketchup
1 Tbsp. Worcestershire Sauce

Combine all ingredients in baking dish, mix well. Bake at 350° for 20 minutes or until bubbly.

Blackeyed Peas

Lee English from The English Family Recipe Treasury

1 lb blackeyed peas
1 onion chopped
1 stalk celery chopped
1/3 pimento pepper chopped
3 cans chicken broth
1 bay leaf
1/4 lemon squeezed
1/4 tsp garlic salt
1/2 tsp beau monde or celery salt
salt & black pepper to taste
1/3 c chopped ham
1/2 c chopped canned tomatoes

Soak peas overnight, drain & wash. Saute' onions, pepper & celery in 3 T oil or bacon grease. Add seasonings, tomatoes, broth, & 2 c water. Heat then add peas, lemon juice & ham. Bring to a boil & then simmer for 4 hrs.

Butternut Squash Risotto

Annette Ahart, Vince's Family from 2008 Ahart Family Reunion Cookbook

4 cups chicken broth
2 Tbsp olive oil
1 large onion, finely chopped
1/2 tsp salt
1/4 tsp black pepper
2 Tbsp finely chopped fresh sage
1 small butternut squash
1 large clove of garlic, finely chopped
1-1/2 cups Arborio rice
1 cup dry white wine
1/2 cup (2 oz) grated Parmesan cheese

Peel, seed and grate squash (about 4 cups). Warm chicken broth in small saucepan over low heat. Heat olive oil in large saucepan over medium heat. Add onion, salt, and pepper to oil and cook for 1 minute. Add squash, sage. and garlic to onions. Cook until squash begins to soften, about 3 minutes. Add rice to squash mixture and cook stirring constantly for 3 minutes. Add wine to rice and squash and cook, stirring frequently, until the liquid is absorbed. Add broth to rice and squash, about 1/2 cup at a time, stirring occasionally and waiting until the liquid is absorbed before adding more. It should take about 30 minutes for all the broth to be absorbed. Remove from heat and stir in the Parmesan cheese.

Serve immediately, or cool and reheat to serve later. This makes great leftovers.

Candy Yams Soufflé

Dawn-Marie Sneed from Dawn-Marie's Favorite Family and Cookbook Recipes

4 medium sweet potatoes (2 lbs)
1/2 c. (1 stick) butter
3/4 c. sugar
1/2 c. firmly packed brown sugar
1 T. fresh lemon juice
1/4 c. milk
2 T. cornstarch
1 tsp. ground nutmeg
1 tsp. vanilla extract
2 c. mini marshmallows

Preheat the oven to 350ºF. Grease a 1-1/2 quart casserole dish. Peel and cut the sweet potatoes into large chunks. In a 4-quart pot of boiling water, cook the potatoes until tender, for 20 to 30 minutes. Drain. Return the drained potatoes to the saucepan, but not the heat. Stir in the butter until melted and the potatoes are mashed. Stir in both sugars and the lemon juice. In a small bowl, stir together the milk, cornstarch, nutmeg, and vanilla. Stir into the potatoes. Spoon into the prepared casserole dish.

Bake for 1 hour. Sprinkle the marshmallows over the top and let bake for 7 to 10 minutes longer or until the marshmallows are melted and brown.

Caramelized Vidalia Onion

Tom Sauvageau from The Sauvageau Family Cookbook

1 tsp butter
1 tsp beef bouillon (or 2 cubes)
1 tsp brown sugar
1 Vidalia onion (or Walla Walla or Washington sweet onion)

Cut hole in top of onion and place all ingredients into center of onion. Bake in microwave until cooked (about 5 minutes).

Vegetables and Vegetarian Dishes

Cheese and Walnut Stuffed Peppers

Rachel Bjerke from The Schuldt Family Cookbook

6 large green peppers
4 med. onions, chopped
butter
2 c. brown rice, cooked
1 c. finely chopped walnuts
1/2 lb. cheddar cheese, grated
4 eggs, beaten
2 tsp. caraway seeds
sea salt

Preheat oven to 350°. Remove stem caps, pulp, and seeds from peppers. Stir fry onions in butter. Place in large bowl and mix in remaining ingredients. Stuff each pepper as full as possible. Arrange peppers open-end up in a baking dish and pour a little water in the dish. Bake for 30 to 40 minutes or until peppers are tender.

Corn Fritters

Karen Arnold from Goodman Family and Friends Cookbook Favorites

1 1/2 c. cream style corn
2 eggs, lightly beaten
1 cup milk
1 tbsp. sugar
1 1/2 tbsp. baking powder
1/2 tsp. salt
1 1/2 cup flour

Mix ingredients together. Fry by dropping batter with a tablespoon into 1 1/2 inch of hot grease in a frying pan. Fry until golden brown and batter is done in the center of fritter.

Corn Souffle

JoAn Howerton from The Brown Robbins Cookbook

Corn Souffle

2 cans whole kernel corn drained
1 c. shredded cheddar cheese
2 Tbsp. finely chopped onions
1/c. melted butter or margarine
1/4 c. flour
1/4 tsp. salt
1/8 tsp. black pepper
1 cup milk
1 Tbsp. chopped fresh parsley
3 eggs, separated

PREHEAT oven to 350°F. Mix drained corn, cheddar cheese, onions, flour, butter, salt, pepper and milk in medium saucepan. Add egg yolks and mix with all.
BEAT egg whites in small bowl with electric mixer on high speed until stiff peaks form; set aside. Gently stir in egg whites.
SPOON into 1-1/2-qt. casserole dish. Place dish in large baking pan, then place in oven.
BAKE 10 min. at 350°. Lower oven to 325° and bake for additional 40 minutes or until center is set.

Cottonwood Beans

Jean Thayer from Memories of Love, Cooking and Great Smells!

1 lb. Jimmy Dean's low-fat sausage
1 lb. lean ground beef
1 lg. onion, chopped
2 lg. cans Bush's Best baked beans
1 16-oz. can lima beans, drained
1 16-oz. can butter beans, drained
1 can chopped tomatoes
1 Tbsp. liquid smoke flavoring
3 Tbsp. vinegar
Garlic, minced (to taste)
2 sm. cans chili peppers, diced (I use Hatch chilies)

Brown together sausage, beef and onion. Drain fat and add all other ingredients. Simmer for about 8 hours on low in a crock pot.

Cream Potatoes and Kielbasa

Eleanor Wark from McMillan Family and Friends Cookbook

1 (26oz) package frozen hash brown potatoes
1# fully cooked Kielbasa or Polish sausage, cut into 1/4" slices
1 (10 1/4 oz) can condensed cream of mushroom soup, undiluted.
1 Cup shredded cheddar cheese.
1/2 cup water.

In a slow cooker, combine all ingredients. Cover and cook on low for 6 to 8 hours or until the potatoes are tender. This is a very easy recipe, for working gals, just throw it in the crock pot and forget it!

Creole Roasted Yams

Holly Magner from The Zuelke Family Cookbook

5 pounds yams
1/4 c. olive oil
1 T. paprika
1 T. ground coriander
1 T. minced garlic
1 T. sea salt
1 T. crushed red chili pepper flakes
1 t. cayenne

Preheat oven to 350°.
Scrub yams clean. Slice yams into wedges that are about 4 inches long and 1/2-1 in. wide. Mix olive oil and spices together in a large bowl to make a paste. Toss yams in spice mixture until evenly coated. Spread yams onto 2 parchment lined cookie sheets in a single layer. Roast in oven for about 20-25 minutes, then stir and roast 10-20 minutes more until yams are tender and have a slightly crispy skin.

Eggplant Parmesan

Mario & Jo Anne Monaco from The Rogers' Girls Family Cookbook

Monaco Tomato Sauce
2 medium size eggplant
2 Eggs and a little water
Italian style bread crumbs
Olive oil
1 lb Sliced mozzarella cheese
Grated Parmesan cheese

Cut eggplant into 1/4 inch slices. Coat each slice (both sides) with Italian style bread crumbs and egg mixture. Cook in olive oil. Do not over cook. Add oil as needed (both sides). When browned and tender, place on paper towels.

In a 4 quart casserole, line the bottom of the pan with sauce. Add cooked eggplant, some sauce, slice of mozzarella cheese and cover with sauce. Add parmesan cheese.

Repeat with layers of eggplant, etc. Bake at 375° over for about 40 to 50 minutes or until bubbly & tender.

Eggplant Spaghetti Sauce Supreme

Annie Laurie Cisneros from Joy of the Repast: Favorite Recipes of Family and Friends

1/4 cup olive oil
1 large eggplant (about 1 1/2 pounds) cut into cubes
3 medium onions, coarsely chopped
3 cloves garlic, minced
1 large green pepper, chopped
2 (1 pound) cans crushed tomatoes (or whole and whirl in the blender)
2 tsp. Sucanat (I use brown sugar)
1 tbsp. dried basil
1/2 cup chopped fresh parsley
1 small can sliced ripe olives, drained (optional)
1/4 tsp. salt
1/4 tsp. pepper
I lb. pasta of your choice

Heat oil in a large soup kettle over medium heat. Add eggplant and onions. Reduce heat, cover and cook, stirring often, until eggplant is soft and lightly browned, about 25 minutes.
Add garlic and bell pepper. Cook for 2 minutes, stirring occasionally.
Stir in tomatoes and their liquid. Stir in Sucanat (sugar) and basil.
Lower heat, cover and simmer for 15 minutes, stirring occasionally.
Stir in parsley, olives, salt and pepper. Simmer uncovered, stirring often until sauce thickens, about 20 minutes (or more). Serve over pasta or use for a lasagna or pizza sauce.

German Potato Salad

Gumma from Roebken Family Cookbook

3 lb new potatoes
5 slices bacon
1 heaping T flour
1/2 c vinegar
1/2 c sugar
1 1/2 c water
1/2 onion cut up
 (I like to use green onions about 1/2 c)

Cook potatoes whole. Cool. Dice bacon and fry until brown. Remove bacon from drippings and set aside. Add flour to drippings and mix well, then add vinegar, sugar and water. Cook over medium heat until thickened. Assemble in bowl in alternating layers: potatoes, bacon, onion, salt and pepper and sauce. Repeat layers. Stir lightly. Serve warmed or cold.

Gluten Free Scalloped Potatoes

Sabreena Rabun from The Wellness Cookbook

4 tbsp. (1/2 Stick) butter
1/2 cup rice flour
3/4 C. Milk
White Pepper
Dash Kosher Salt or Sea Salt
3/4 C Shredded Cheddar Cheese
Potatoes, peeled and thinly sliced

Preheat oven to 350 degrees F. Lightly grease an oven safe baking dish with butter. Melt butter in saucepan. Gradually add flour to make a blond roux, then slowly add the milk and allow the mixture to thicken. Layer potatoes, sauce, and shredded cheese for a total of about three layers. Bake covered for about 45 minutes to an hour, removing the cover the last 10 minutes. Potatoes are done when they are tender. Let stand a few minutes before serving.

Granny's Sweet Potato Crisp

Glenna Crum from Favorite Recipes

6 medium sweet potatoes
1/4 c. flour
1 1/2 tsp. fresh ground pepper
1/4 c. finely chopped pecans
1/2 c. margarine
1/2 c. firmly packed brown sugar
1/4 c. evaporated milk

Cook whole potatoes in boiling water until tender. Peel and slice crosswise into 1/2" thick pieces. Spread into shallow, buttered 1 1/2 quart casserole pan. Cut margarine into flour and brown sugar until mix resembles coarse crumbs. Add pepper, milk, and pecans. Mix well and spread over potatoes. Place under broiler, about 6" from heat, until bubbly - about 6 minutes.

Honey-Pecan-Yam (Sweet Potato) Souffle

June Seidl - First Solar from The Toledo Area Chapter APA Celebrates National Payroll Week!

1 tsp salt
1 1/2 cups light cream or Half & Half
1/2 cup honey
2 Tbsp cornstarch
3 eggs (beaten)
3/4 cups chopped pecans
2 cups cooked yams or sweet potatoes (mashed)

Pre-heat oven to 325 Throughly mix all ingredients in the order given. Pour in a greased 10" x 6" or 8" x 8" baking dish Bake for 50 - 60 minutes until knife inserted in center comes out clean.

Personal Notes: Making this recipe was the only way my mother could get my sister, brother, and me to eat sweet potatoes. Now it is a family favorite for Thanksgiving dinner.

Judy's Chili Rellenos

Linda Knudsen from The Jones-Simpson Cookbook

Eggs
Flour
Monterey Jack Cheese
Cooking Oil
Whole Green Chilies, Roasted, Peeled & Seeded

This is truly a recipe that you don't measure the ingredients. Figure 2-3 Rellenos per person. For approximately 12 Chilies, mix 2 eggs with enough flour to make a fairly thick batter. Fill each chili with a strip of Monterey Jack cheese. Put enough oil in a heavy skillet to cover the chilies about half way up. Dip each filled chili in the batter covering well. Then drop in the hot oil. Fry until golden brown and turn to fry other side. Enjoy!

Lee's Famous Cole Slaw

Lee Kleinman from The Kleinman Family Cookbook

8 oz. bag red cabbage
8 oz. bag green cabbage
1 bunch green onions
1 red pepper
1 green pepper
8 oz jar green olives with pimento
12 oz bottle Italian dressing

Remove stem and seeds from peppers, slice thin and cut into bite size pieces, about 2 inches long. Wash and cut green onions into small rounds including greens. Coarsely chop olives. (you may use "salad olives"). Mix cabbage, peppers, onions and olives in a large bowl. Add Italian dressing and mix.

Personal Notes: I prefer Seven Seas or Wishbone Italian dressing because they are not sweet. You may soak the cabbage in ice cold water for a few hours to crisp it up. Use a salad spinner to remove excess water.

Louisiana Yam and Coconut Casserole

Lynn Spataro from McKee Cooks

2 16 oz. cans Louisiana yams, drained
2 eggs
1/4 c. butter, melted
1/2 c. brown sugar
1/2 c. walnuts or pecans, chopped
3/4 t. salt
1/4 t. cinnamon
1 t. vanilla extract
2/3 c. shredded coconut
1 T. butter, melted

Mash yams in large mixing bowl. Add eggs, butter, sugar, salt, nuts, cinnamon and vanilla extract. Beat until mixture is light and fluffy. Turn into a greased, shallow casserole or 1-quart baking dish. Bake at 325°F for 35 minutes. Toss coconut with butter. Sprinkle a border of coconut around edge of casserole. Bake 10-15 minutes until coconut is lightly browned.

Onion Casserole

Jeannine Ball from Cookin' with Balls II

1 egg, beaten
1 cup heavy cream
3/4 tsp salt
1/2 tsp ground black pepper
1/2 cup shredded Cheddar cheese
Paprika
1lb. sweet onions sliced into rings and separated (Vidalia or other type of sweet onions)

Place onion slices in a med. saucepan; cover wth water & bring to a boil. Boil for 1 minute. Drain onions; transfer to an 8-inch square baking dish. In a small bowl combine egg, cream, salt & pepper; pour mixture over onions. Sprinkle with cheese and paprika. Bake for 25 minutes at 350 degrees.

Onion Fritters

Aunt Flossie from Grammy's Family Cookbook

3/4 c all-purpose flour
4 Tbsp cornmeal
2 tsp baking powder
1/2 tsp salt
1/2 c milk
1 large onion - diced
Canola or other vegetable oil, for deep-frying

Place flour, cornmeal, baking powder, and salt in a large bowl and mix. Pour milk into the flour mixture and mix until just blended; do not overmix. Stir in the diced onions and let the batter rest for 10 - 30 minutes. It should be slightly thicker than heavy cream. If it isn't, sprinkle in a little more flour. If it's too thick, add a little more milk. Preheat the oven to its lowest setting. Pour vegetable oil to a depth of 3 inches into a large, heavy saucepan and heat to 375°F on a deep-fry thermometer. Drop the onion fritter batter into the hot oil by the tablespoonful, a few at a time, and fry, turning once, until the fritters are golden brown on both sides, about 3 minutes in all. Check a fritter by breaking it open to see if the center is cooked; if it still seems unset, cook 1 minute more. Drain on paper towels. Place the fritters in the oven to keep warm while you finish frying them all.

Parmesan Zucchini

Gloria Cody from All My Children Gotta Eat

1 small red pepper, chopped
1 small onion, chopped
4 small zucchini, thinly sliced
1/2 c. spaghetti sauce
3/4 c. mozzarella cheese, shredded
2 tbsp. grated Parmesan cheese

Cook and stir peppers and onions in large nonstick skillet sprayed with cooking spray on medium heat for 5 min. Add zucchini; cook and stir 2 min.
Stir in spaghetti sauce; cover and cook for 8 minutes, or until vegetables are crisp-tender, stirring occasionally.
Sprinkle with cheese; cook, covered for about a minute or until cheese is melted.

Pasta with Mushrooms and Goat Cheese

Amy Aaland from The Vreeland Family Cookbook Project

3/4 lb Penne pasta
10 oz white mushrooms, sliced
1 large onion, diced
4 cloves garlic, minced
5 oz goat cheese
2 tsp. Italian seasonings
1/2 cup toasted pecan pieces
2 tbsp. cilantro, minced
olive oil
salt and pepper
10 oz assorted exotic mushrooms (portabella, cremini, etc.,) sliced

Cook the pasta in salted boiling water until al dente. While the pasta is cooking, put olive oil, onion, garlic and a little salt in saute pan. Saute until onions are soft, about 5 minutes. Add mushrooms and a touch more salt. Cook until brown. Add the Marsala wine to get any brownings off the bottom of the pan and then add the Italian seasonings. Put Pasta in large serving bowl with about 1/2 cup of the liquid it cooked in. Add the mushrooms, pecans and goat cheese. Toss. Add the cilantro and pepper and toss again.

Potato Bacon Casserole

Jo Anne Johnson Cunningham from The Snyder/Johnson Family Cookbook Project

1/2 cup sweet onion - chopped
8 oz. bacon - fried & crumbled
1 cup shredded mild cheddar cheese
1 can evaporated milk
1 egg
1 1/2 tsp. Morton's Seasoning Blend
4 cups frozen shredded hash brown potatoes

Preheat oven to 350°. Grease 1 1/2 quart casserole dish. Layer 1/2 potatoes, onions, bacon, cheese then repeat. Mix together milk, egg, and seasoning. Pour over top the potato mixture. Bake @ for 55/60 minutes.

Potato Wedges that Kick

Mitchell Chester from The New Donovan Family Cookbook Volume II

5-8 Russet Potatoes
1/4 cup + - canola oil
4-5 garlic cloves
Red pepper flakes
Salt & Fresh Ground Pepper

Scrub and cut potatoes in steak fry sized wedges skin on. Soak in cold water for an hour or warm water for 15 minutes sirring occasionally. Drain well. Squeeze garlic into oil and add some salt. Coat potatoes and let them sit for a few minutes. Spread on a cookie pan and liberally salt, pepper, and shake on red pepper flakes to taste. Make certain to coat all sides of the spuds. The red pepper flakes are key to the flavor theme. Seal the top with foil and place in a 475 degree oven on bottom rack for 15 minutes. Remove foil, flip, re-salt, and lower temp to 450 and bake for another 20-30 minutes or until visibly browned.

Roasted Cauliflower with Brown Butter and Sage

Diana Terlato from 'We Love You Alison' Cookbook

1 head Cauliflower
4 T. unsalted butter
2 T. olive oil
2 T. chopped fresh sage leaves
sea salt and pepper to taste

1. Preheat oven to 400° F.
2. Place cauliflower on baking sheet with sides.
3. Melt the butter in a pan, over medium heat for 2 - 4 minutes until brown. It will start to give off a nutty aroma. If it burns, start over.
4. Add the sage to the butter then the oil. Toss over the cauliflower and season with salt and pepper.
4. Roast the cauliflower for 30 to 35 minutes, tossing half way through.

Roasted Potatoes with Artichokes & Feta

Carol Lewis Foster from Lewis Girl's Lucky Duck Cookbook

2 lb. small red potatoes, quartered
2 14 oz. cans artichoke hearts, drained and halved
2 T. fresh thyme or 2 tsp. dried
1 T. olive oil
1/2 tsp. salt, kosher preferred
1/2 tsp. black pepper
1/2 c. feta cheese, crumbled

Preheat oven 425°
Coat 9 x 13" pan with cooking spray. Combine all ingredients, except feta, in pan. Cook 40 minutes or until tender. Add cheese and toss gently.

Sinful Potatoes

Sarah Watson from The McCullough Family Cookbook

1 lb. sliced bacon
3 lbs. red potatoes
1/2 tbsp. liquid crab boil
1/2 lb. Velveeta cheese, cubed
1 cup sour cream
3 green onions, chopped
1 stick butter
Salt and pepper to taste

Cook the bacon in a skillet until crisp and crumble into small pieces. Cut the red potatoes into quarters, leaving the skins on. Place in large saucepan of boiling water. Add the liquid crab boil and cook until the potatoes are tender. Drain. Add bacon, Velveeta cheese, sour cream, green onions and butter. Stir until the red potatoes are mashed. Season with salt and pepper.

Southern Fried Green Tomatoes

Debbie Hanson, wife of Jim Hanson from Hanson Family Cookbook

Fresh green tomatoes
Flour
Salt
Pepper
Vegtable oil

Slice tomatoes about 1/4". Spread on plate. Sprinkle salt evenly over tomatoes. Continue placing tomato slices in layer over previous layer and sprinkle with salt until all tomatoes have been salted. Let the Tomatoes sit at room temperature or in refrigerator for at least 2 hours (Important). This removes water from tomatoes so that they will cook up nice and crispy.

Remove tomatoes from container. Mix flour, a little salt and pepper in a bowl. Coat each tomato slice with flour mixture. Heat oil in a skillet to medium high. Place tomatoes in oil. (Reduce heat when necessary). Let tomatoes brown on one side, then turn and brown on the other side. When tomatoes are a golden brown, remove one at a time and place on paper towels to drain.

Spicy Shrimp Stuffed Mirliton

Harriet Duhe' Melancon from A Taste of Our Family

3 mirlitons
2 tablespoons olive oil
1/2 cup chopped onions
1/4 cup chopped bell pepper
1/4 cup chopped celery
2 teaspoons minced shallots
1 teaspoon minced garlic
1/2 pound large shrimp
1/2 cup dried fine bread crumbs
2 tablespoons finely chopped parsley
Salt and cayenne
1/4 cup grated Parmigiano-Reggiano cheese, plus 2 tablespoons for garnish

Boil mirlitons, cut in half and remove seeds. Peel and devein shrimp. Cut each into 3 pieces.

Preheat the oven to 350 degrees. Scoop out the pulp of the mirlitons, leaving a 1/4-inch shell. Reserve the pulp.

In a saute pan, heat the olive oil. Saute the onions, peppers, celery, and shallots for about 5 minutes, or until they are wilted and golden. Season with salt and cayenne. Add the garlic, shrimp and reserved pulp. Saute the mixture for 5 minutes. Stir in the bread crumbs, cheese, and parsley. Remove from the heat. Fill each mirliton shell with the mixture. Bake for 1 hour. Place the stuffed mirlitons on a platter. Garnish with cheese.

Sweet Potato Pie

Anne McCarthy from McCarthy Family Cookbook

4 cans (29 oz) cut sweet potatoes
2 cans (14 oz) sweetened condensed milk
1 stick of butter (softened)
3/4 c. brown sugar
3/4 c. crushed corn flakes
3/4 c. chopped pecans
1 stick of butter (softened)

Combine sweet potatoes, milk and one stick of butter and whip until good and fluffy; set aside. Blend brown sugar, corn flakes, pecans and butter together in a separate bowl. Then place half the corn flake mixture on the bottom of a 9" x 13" glass casserole pan that is well coated with Pam cooking spray. Spread the sweet potato mixture over top of this crust, then top with the remaining corn flake mixture. Bake at 350° F for forty minutes.

Texas Potatoes

Nancy Alvord from Family Recipes To Remember

1-2lb. bag frozen Hash Browns
1/2 cup Butter
1/2 cup chopped Onion
2 cups Sour Cream
1 can Cream of Chicken Soup
2 tsp. Salt
1/2 tsp. Pepper
2 cups Corn Flakes crushed
1/4 cup Butter

Mix all ingredients together except the last 2 listed. Put into a 9 X 13 baking dish. Top with corn flakes and dot with butter. Bake uncovered at 350° for 45 minutes.

Tomato Pie

Linda Segebrecht from The Wiersch Family Cookbook

1 ½ c. Bisquick
½ c. milk
7 medium tomatoes
Garlic salt
Lemon pepper
Basil
Chives or green onion
1 c. mayo
1 c. cheddar cheese
1 small chopped onion
Salt and pepper to taste

Blanch tomatoes in boiling water to remove skins, drain and slice. Pat dry between paper towels after sliced.

Preheat oven to 400. For crust, mix Bisquick and milk until paste forms. Put ball between wax paper, flatten, place into bottom of pie tin or small baking dish. Bake for 5 minutes. Layer tomatoes on top of crust and sprinkle with all seasonings. Mix mayo, cheese, onion, salt, pepper together and layer on top. Bake for 30 minutes or until bubbly.

Vegetables with Cheese

Sue Chappell from The Chappell Hodge Family Cookbook

1 1/2 c. broccoli florets
1 1/2 c. cauliflower florets
1 c. fresh mushrooms, sliced
1 medium onion, chopped
3 carrots, sliced
1 large tomato, diced
2/3 c. dry white wine
3 garlic cloves, minced
2 tbsp. olive oil
12-16 oz. sliced Muenster cheese

In a large saute pan, heat olive oil over medium-high heat. Add onions and garlic and saute until onions are translucent. Add broccoli, carrots, and cauliflower and saute 3 minutes or until vegetables are crisp-tender. Add mushrooms and cook another minute. Add tomatoes and wine and bring to a boil. Cook about another 2 minutes. Using a slotted spoon, transfer vegetable mixture to a 9x13 inch baking pan and layer cheese over top. Broil on high just until cheese melts and starts to brown. Remove from oven and serve immediately. Can be used as a main dish or a side dish.

Veggie Pancotta

Stephanie Esposito (Bartocetti) from La Famiglia Campano

1 loaf slightly stale Italian bread, cubed
3 garlic cloves, minced
1 can vegetable or chicken stock
2 cans artichoke hearts, chopped
2 packages frozen whole leaf spinach
2 cups chopped roasted red peppers
1/2 cup black olives, sliced
1/2 cup Parmesan cheese, grated plus additional for topping

Thaw and squeeze dry spinach. In large bowl, combine bread, garlic, and vegetables. Toss to combine. Pour in stock, enough to saturate the bread. Let sit for about 10-15 minutes to absorb. Add cheese and stir gently. Pour into large greased casserole dish and sprinkle with additional cheese. Bake at 350 for approx 30 minutes. (covered for 20 mins, then uncovered for additional 10 minutes)

Zelda's Potatoes

Nancy Atwell from Four Generations of Johnson Women

1 2-lb package of frozen hash browns
1/2 cup chopped onions
2 cans cream of chicken soup
1 pint sour cream
8 oz cream cheese (softened)
1 tsp. salt
1 1/2 tsp. pepper
1 1/2 cups crushed corn flakes
1/2 cup melted butter

Mix all ingredients (except corn flakes and butter) and spread in a 13x9x2 pan. Place corn flakes and butter in a ziplock bag, squeeze out the air and crush with a rolling pin. Sprinkle on top of potatoes. Bake uncovered 1 hour at 350º.

Desserts, Pies Cakes and Cookies

Mama's Oatmeal Cookies pg. 152

Rollout Cookies pg. 157

Almond Butter Crunch

Mom from Mom's Recipe Box

1 cup butter
1 1/3 cups sugar
1 tbsp light corn syrup
3 tbsp water
1 cup finely chopped toasted almonds
1 cup broken or chopped toasted blanched almonds
4-4 1/2-oz bars milk chocolate, melted

Melt butter in large saucepan. Add sugar, corn syrup and water. Cook, stirring occasionally, to hard-crack stage, watch mixture very closely when it begins to boil. When mixture reaches hard-crack stage, quickly stir in coarsely chopped almonds; spread in 13 x 9" pan. Cool thoroughly. Turn out on waxed paper; spread top with half the melted chocolate and half the finely chopped almonds. Cover with waxed paper, turn over and spread other side with remaining chocolate and nuts. Break in pieces...and watch it disappear!

Angel Pie

Recipe Hall of Fame Dessert Cookbook from The Vold Family Cookbook Project

Meringue:
4 egg whites
1/4 tsp. cream of tartar
1 c. sugar
Pinch of salt
1 tsp. vanilla
Filling:
4 egg yolks
1/2 c. sugar
1/4 c. lemon juice (fresh squeezed)
2 tbsp. grated lemon peel
2 c. whipping cream, whipped, divided
Toasted almonds for garnish

For meringue: Preheat oven to 275°. Beat egg whites until frothy. Add cream of tartar and beat until stiff, gradually adding sugar and salt. Fold in vanilla. Spread in a 9 in. buttered pie pan covering bottom and sides; shape with the back of a spoon, making the bottom 1/4 in. thick and the sides 1 in. thick. Bake for 1 hour; leave in the oven to cool for 1 hour.
For filling: Beat egg yolks until lemon-colored, gradually adding sugar, lemon juice and peel. Cook in the top of a double boiler over hot water (not touching pan) until thick, stirring constantly. Cool. Fold in half of whipped cream. Spread over meringue and cover with remaining whipped cream. Sprinkle toasted almonds over the top. Refrigerate. May be made the day before.

Ashtalia

Sheila Rich from The Baptist Heritage Cookbook

7 c. milk
1 T. rose water
1 c. cornstarch
slices of bread
4 c. water
2 c. sugar
1 T. rose water
1 T. orange blossom water
Place milk, cornstarch and 1 T. rose water in saucepan and bring to a boil while stirring constantly. Remove from

heat. Toast bread lightly. Fit the toasted slices into a flat pan (a 13 X 9 pan works well, or a flat-bottomed casserole dish). This will be your crust! Pour the cooked milk mixture over the layer of toast and even it out. Chill in the fridge. Mix the syrup ingredients (4 c. water, 2 c. sugar, 1 T. rose water) in a saucepan and bring to a boil. Boil to a thread stage. Remove from heat and allow to cool.

When ready to serve, cut the Ashtalia into squares and place on dessert plates. Spoon some syrup over each serving and top with chopped pistachio nuts.

Bailey's Irish Cream Cookies

Naomi Jones from The Jones-Simpson Cookbook

1/2 Cup Butter
1/2 Cup Brown Sugar
1/2 Cup Granulated Sugar
1 Tsp. Vanilla
1 Egg
1/2 Cup Bailey's Irish Cream
2 1/4 Cups Cake Flour
1/2 tsp. Soda
1/2 tsp. Salt
3/4 Cup Coconut
1/2 Cup Chopped Pecans
1 lb. Package Chocolate Chips

Cream butter, sugar and egg until fluffy, add vanilla & Irish Cream. Mix dry ingredients, blend with creamed mixture. Add nuts, coconut and chips. Drop by teaspoon onto un-greased baking sheet. Bake 375º for 8-10 minutes. Cool.

Blitz Torte

Gumma from Roebken Family Cookbook

3/4 c shortening
3/4 c sugar
6 egg yolks
1/2 c milk
1 1/2 c cake flour
1 1/2 tsp baking powder
6 egg whites
1 1/2 c sugar for meringue
1/2 tsp vanilla
unblanched almond chips
Vanilla custard or cooked pudding

Cream shortening and sugar, add egg yolks and beat well. Add dry ingredients alternately with milk. Pour into 2 greased 9" cake pans. Beat 6 egg whites until stiff. Gradually add 1 1/2 c sugar and then vanilla. Spread meringue over batter. Bake at 350º for 25-30 min. Place one layer on serving plate, and cover with custard. Top with second layer.

Blueberry Jello Dessert

Karen Rankin from The Rankin Family Cookbook Project

6 oz box raspberry jello
2 cup boiling water
1 can blueberry pie filling
1 cup light sour cream
8 ounces light cream cheese
1 tsp vanilla
1/4 cup sugar
1 large can crushed pineapple with juice

Dissolve jello in boiling water. Put in Refrigerator to set. Beat topping ingredients until fluffy and spread over set jello mixture. Chill and serve

Butter Tarts

Tyler's favorite! from 5 o:clock...Suppers Ready!

1/3 cup butter
1/2 cup corn syrup
1/2 cup light brown sugar
4 Tbsp. whipping cream
1/2 tsp. salt
2 eggs, slightly beaten

Melt butter, add syrup, sugar, and salt. Mix well. When cool add the eggs. Line the tart pan with the pastry. Sprinkle with raisins in bottom of the tart shells. Pour in the liquid.
Bake until nicely brown in a 400° oven for 20 mins.

Chess Pie

Vara Wallace from A Real Southern Comfort

1 1/2 cups sugar
2 tbsp flour
1 stick melted butter
3 eggs yolks and 1 whole egg beaten
1 tsp vanilla flavoring

Mix all ingredients and pour into unbaked pie shell and bake in 300 degree oven until custard is set.

Desserts, Pies, Cakes and Cookies

Choco-holic Cake

Nancy Alvord from Family Recipes To Remember

1 pkg. Chocolate Cake Mix
1 -3.4oz.pkg. Chocolate instant pudding
1 cup Milk
1/2 cup Sour Cream
4 Eggs
1 cup chopped Walnuts
2 cups Chocolate Chips
Unsweetened Chocolate Baking Bar
3 T. Butter
2-3 T. Water
1 tsp. Vanilla
1/2 cup powdered sugar

Combine cake mix, pudding mix, milk, sour cream and eggs in large mixer bowl. Beat on low speed just until blended. Beat on high speed for 2 minutes. Stir in choc. chips and nuts. Pour into a greased and floured bundt pan. Bake for 55-65 minutes. Cool for 20 minutes. For glaze melt chocolate and butter in saucepan over low heat. Stir until smooth. Remove from heat. Stir in powdered sugar alternately with water until of desired consistency. Stir in vanilla. Pour glaze over cake.

Chocolate Peanut Butter Fudge (Tim's Favorite)

Karen Malone from Recipes from Nannie Karen's Kitchen

4 cups sugar
4 Tbsp. cocoa
1 cup milk
1 tsp. vanilla
1\2 cup butter
1\2 cup peanut butter

Boil sugar, cocoa and milk for no more than 8-10 minutes. Remove from heat and stir in vanilla, butter and peanut butter pour in greased 12x8 pan. Let cool. Cut into squares.

Chocolate Chip Pie

Marilyn Dakan from The Ward/Bagley/Blevins and Friends Family Cookbook

1/2 lb marshmallows
1/2 c milk
8 oz cream cheese
1 c heavy whipping cream
pkg chocolate chips
graham cracker crust

Slowly heat 1/2 pound marshmallows and 1/2 cup milk.
In a separate bowl whip 1 cup heavy whipping cream. When whipped add 8 oz soft cream cheese. Add to marshmallows and milk mixture. Allow to cool. Once cool add a package of chocolate chips. Pour into graham cracker crust. Refrigerate.

Chocolate Covered Cherries

Susan Privot from Family Recipes

3 tbsp butter, softened
3 tbsp light corn syrup
1/4 tsp salt
2 c confectioners sugar
1/2 milk and 1/2 dark chocolate
1 - 16 oz jar maraschino cherries with stems, drained and dry (reserved juice)

Combine butter, syrup, salt and powdered sugar in bowl. Add enough cherry juice to make a dough. Form into a ball, wrap in plastic and chill 1-2 hours. Take marble sized piece of dough, flatten it out and wrap around each cherry. Put on wax paper lined cookie sheet, chill 1-2 hours till firm. Melt candy over low heat. Holding stems, dip each cherry into coating and set into individual candy wrappers. Chill.

Chocolate Dessert Fondue

Myra Beth Bundy from Cooking With The Cousins

12 (1 oz.) chocolate candy bars, broken
1/4 c. milk
10 large marshmallows
1/4 c. whipping cream

Place chocolate bars and milk in fondue pot. Turn fondue pot temperature to warm. Stirring constantly, add marshmallows until melted. Gradually add whipping cream. Serve with fruit pieces, pound cake or angel food cake.

Personal Notes: We indulge in this treat two times each year. It is a tradition for my family to make this fondue on New Year's Eve. The boys really have a great time with it. Six months later I make it for Gina on her birthday.

Chocolate Éclair Desert

Lee English from The English Family Recipe Treasury

1 lg vanilla instant pudding
1 small Cool Whip
1 can chocolate frosting
Graham crackers

Mix pudding according to package directions. Fold Cool Whip into pudding. Layer graham crackers in bottom of glass dish. Pour a layer of pudding on, then top with crackers, then another layer of pudding. Soften chocolate frosting a bit in the microwave and pour over top of pudding. Chill before serving.

Chocolate Snowflakes

Donnalee (Cater) Geiger from Our Family Favorites Cookbook

2 c flour
2 tsp baking powder
1/2 tsp salt
1/4 c butter
2 c sugar
4 eggs
1/2 c chopped walnuts
powdered sugar
4 squares unsweetened baking chocolate

Sift together flour, baking powder, and salt. Melt the butter and chocolate in a saucepan over low heat. Remove and cool slightly. Blend the 2 c of sugar and eggs together adding the eggs one at a time and beating for one minute. Add the dry ingredients and nuts. Mix well. Chill at least 15 minutes. Shape into small balls using 1 T of dough for each. Roll in powdered sugar. Place on greased baking sheets and bake @ 300 for 12 minutes.

Chocolate Zucchini Cake

Linda Schlais from The Cookbook of Our Favorite Foods and Memories

1/2 C Butter
1/2 C Veggie Oil
1 3/4 C White Sugar
2 Eggs
1/2 C Sour Milk or Buttermilk
1 tsp Vanilla
2 C Flour
1 tsp Baking Soda
1/2 tsp Cinnamon
1/2 tsp Cloves, ground
1/2 tsp Salt
4 T Cocoa
2 1/2 C Grated Zucchini
1/4 C Walnuts, chopped
1/4 C Chocolate Chips

Cream together the oil, butter and sugar. Mix in the eggs, milk and vanilla. In a separate bowl, mix together the flour, soda, cinnamon, cloves, salt and cocoa. Mix together the sugar mixture and the flour mixture. Add the zucchini. Bake in a greased 9 x 13 pan at 325° for 45 minutes. Top with walnuts and chocolate chips.

Cookie Pizza

Mom from Mom's Favorite Recipes

1/2 c. packed brown sugar
1/4 c. sugar
1/2 c. butter or margarine, softened
1 t. vanilla
1 egg
1 1/4 c. flour
1/2 t. baking soda
12 oz mini semi sweet chocolate chips
1 c. whipped topping
1/4 c. nuts, chopped
1/4 c. coconut, toasted
1/2 c. M&M's

Mix sugars, margarine, vanilla and egg in large bowl. Stir in flour and baking soda (dough will be stiff). Stir in chocolate chips. Spread or pat dough in ungreased 12" pizza pan or on a cookie sheet. Bake at 350 for about 15 minutes or until golden brown. Cool in pan. Just before serving, spread cookie with whipped topping. Top with walnuts, coconut and candies. Refrigerate remaining pizza.

Cry Babies

Mom Mom (Clara Hutchison) from Joyce Manwiller's Recipe Box

1 c butter and lard, mixed
1 c sugar
1 c molasses
1 tbsp soda dissolved in 1 c hot water
5 c flour
1 egg
2 tsp cinnamon
2 tsp ginger

Mix and drop by teaspoon onto cookie sheet. Bake at 375 degrees for about 8 to 10 minutes.

Death By Chocolate

Anna Cimillo from Francesco Mattera and Family Recipes

Box of Chocolate Cake Mix
Cup of Kahlua
Box of Instant Chocolate Pudding
Cool Whip
Scores or Heath Candy Bar - Crushed

Follow directions on cake mix and make 2 layers. You will need a Trifle Bowl or a clear bowl big enough to make layers of all ingredients. Put one layer of cake in the bowl. Then pour some of the Kahlua all around on top of it.Then put a layer of Pudding on top of that. Then layer of cool whip. Then a layer of the crushed candy. Continue with all the layers again. You should be able to make two complete layers of all ingredients fit nicely into the bowl.

Devil Dogs

Claire Huckins from Our family and friends cookbook project

6 tbsp. vegetable shortening
1 c. sugar
1 egg
3/4 c. evaporated milk
2 c flour
1 tsp. vanilla
1 tsp. salt
1 tsp. baking powder
1/2 c. instant cocoa

Filling:
1 stick margarine
3/4 c. confectioners sugar
6 tbls. marshmallow fluff
1 tsp. vanilla

Cream sugar, shortening. Add egg and dry ingredients alternately with milk. Mix well. Drop by tsp. on greased cookie sheet. Bake 350° oven for 12 minutes. Cool thoroughly. Beat filling ingredients until light and fluffy. Put filling between two cookies. Enjoy!

Desserts, Pies, Cakes and Cookies

Earthquake Cake

Kathy Pitcher from The McCullough Family Cookbook

1 box German Chocolate Cake Mix
1 1/2 cup shredded coconut
1/2 cup chopped pecans
2 sticks margarine
8 oz cream cheese
1 box confectioners sugar

Grease a deep 9x13 inch pan and preheat oven to 350°. Sprinkle coconut and pecans on bottom of pan. Prepare cake mix as directed on box and pour over coconut & pecans. In bowl, mix margarine and cream cheese with box of powdered sugar. Pour on cake mix but do not mix in. Bake for 40 min. Cool

Fruit Pizza

Elaine Billberg from Memories

2 3/4 cups flour
1/4 tsp. salt
2 tsp. cream of tarter
1 tsp. baking soda
1 1/2 cup sugar
1/2 cup shortening
1/2 cup butter
1 tsp. vanilla
2 eggs
3 oz. cream cheese
1/2 cup sugar
Sliced fresh fruit

Mix together flour, salt, cream of tarter and soda. Cream together 1 cup sugar, shortening and butter. Add vanilla, eggs and dry ingredients. Blend all together and put on pizza pans (lightly flour pan and roll it with rolling pin). Bake crust at 350° until light brown.

Cream cream cheese with 1/2 cup sugar. Spread on cooled crust and top with your favorite fresh fruit such as bananas, strawberries, pineapple, cherries, raspberries, blueberries, kiwi, mandarin oranges.

Fudge Meltaways

Nancy Atwell from Four Generations of Johnson Women

Base:

1/2 c. melted butter
1 square unsweetened chocolate
1/4 c. sugar
1 tsp. vanilla
1 egg, beaten
2 c. graham cracker crumbs
1 c. coconut
1/2 c. chopped pecans

2nd Layer:

2 c. confectioner's sugar
1/4 c. butter
1 tsp. cream or milk (maybe a bit more)
1 tsp. vanilla

Drizzle:

1 1/2 squares unsweetened chocolate

Base: Melt butter and chocolate in top of double boiler, remove from heat and cool. Beat egg in a mixing bowl, add sugar, vanilla, chocolate mixture, coconut, nuts and graham cracker crumbs. Spread this mixture in the bottom of a 13x9x2 pan.

2nd Layer: Cream butter and sugar. Add vanilla and milk to make a thick frosting. If too thick to spread, add more milk. If too thin, add more confectioner's sugar. Spread this frosting over the base layer. Refrigerate to set.

Melt final 1 1/2 squares of chocolate and drizzle over the frosting. Return to refrigerator to set. Cut into small squares (a little of this goes a long way!) and store in tightly covered container. Because egg is never fully cooked, I recommend refrigerating at all times.

Ginger-Pear Cheesecake

Wendy Lotze from Favorite Recipes

1/4 lb lightly salted butter
1 c. finely ground ginger snap cookies
1 c. finely ground vanilla wafers
1/4 c. sugar
2 lbs cream cheese
1 1/2 c. sugar
2 dried pears
1 1/2 tbsp cognac
2 chunks of crystallized ginger, sliced thin
1/2 tsp. vanilla
pinch of salt
4 large eggs
2 c. sour cream
1/4 c. sugar
1/2 tsp. cognac
1/2 tsp. vanilla
3 drops ginger extract
1 chunk crystallized ginger cut into 12 slices

Soak dried pears in 3 tbsp cognac for 2 hours then cut into slices.

Melt butter over low heat. Mix with ginger snap cookies, vanilla wafers and 1/4 c. sugar until well blended. Press mixture over bottom and up sides of a 10" Springform pan.

Combine cream cheese and 1 1/2 c. sugar and beat for 2 minutes or until soft. Add pears, cognac, ginger, vanilla and salt, mixing on low (to prevent air bubbles). Pour filling into crust and bake in preheated 350° oven for 45 minuets. Remove while topping is prepared.

Combine sour cream, 1/4 c. sugar, 1/2 tsp. cognac and extracts in a plastic bowl with spatula. Spread evenly over top of baked filling. Arrange ginger slices. Return to 350° oven for 10 minutes. Remove and immediately place in refrigerator to prevent cracks.

Gluten Free Flourless Peanut Butter Cookies

Sabreena Rabun from The Wellness Cookbook

1 cup Peanut Butter
1 cup White Sugar
1 egg

Preheat oven to 350 degrees F. (180 degrees C). Combine ingredients in a mixing bowl then drop by teaspoonfuls on a cookie sheet. Bake for 8 minutes. Let cool.

Gramma's Fluffy Ruffles (Lemon Jello Dessert)
Dawn-Marie Sneed from Dawn-Marie's Favorite Family and Cookbook Recipes

1 sm.pkg. lemon jello
1 c. hot water
1 can of evaporated milk
1/2 tsp. vanilla
2/3 c. sugar
1 fresh lemon or lemon juice
1 fresh whole grated lemon
12 honey graham crackers, crumbled

Refrigerate evaporated milk for 2 hrs. or put in the freezer for 10 min. Dissolve jello in water, add grated lemon and juice in a bowl. Place mixture in refrigerator for 10 minutes until it thickens like syrup. Pour evaporated milk in a separate bowl and whip until fluffy. Pour jello mixture into the whipped evaporated milk, stirring with a whipper. Spread crackers on bottom of casserole dish, saving some of the top of the dessert. Pour the mixture on top of the crackers. Smooth out mixture and top with the rest of crackers. Garnish with Kiwi, Strawberries, Blueberries or any other fruit.

Hawaiian Pie
Maleah Snipes from The Snipes Family Cookbook Project

1 pre-made graham cracker crust
1 16 oz. can of crushed pineapple
1 box of Jell-O Vanilla Pudding
1 cup sour cream
1 1/4 cup whip cream
1 cup toasted coconut

In a medium bowl, mix vanilla pudding, sour cream, and whip cream together. Mix well but don't over mix. Add pineapple with the juices, fold into pudding mix. Once combined, pour into graham cracker crust. Spread toasted coconut over the top carefully. Loosely cover and refrigerate 2-3 hours or until firm.

Hummingbird Cake
Sue Snyder/Jones from The Snyder/Johnson Family Cookbook Project

3 c all purpose flour
2 c sugar
1 tsp salt
1 tsp baking soda
1 tsp ground cinnamon
3 eggs lightly beaten
1 1/2 cup cooking oil
1 1/2 tsp vanilla
8 oz can crushed pineapple in heavy syrup
1 c chopped pecans
2 c chopped bananas
1/2 c coconut
1 8 oz. softened cream cheese
1 stick softened butter
1 box powdered sugar
1 tsp vanilla
1 cup chopped pecans

Preheat oven to 350 degrees. Prepare three 9 inch cake pans with shortening and flour. Combine dry ingredients in a large bowl. Add eggs and oil. Stir but do not beat. Add pineapple, pecans, coconut, and bananas. Stir until mixed. Do not beat. Pour into prepared cake pans. Bake 25-30 minutes at 350. Cool in pans 10 minutes. Remove and cool completely before icing.

Frosting:
Cream cream cheese. Beat cream cheese, butter, powdered sugar, and 1 tsp vanilla until light and fluffy. Add pecans and spread between layers, on top and sides. Dust the top with fine chopped pecans.

Jessie's Deep Dish Brownies

Jessie Richart from The Warner Family and Friends' Cookbook

3/4 c flour
1/2 c baking cocoa
1/2 tsp salt
1/2 tsp baking powder
3/4 c butter or margerine (1 1/2 sticks)
1 1/2 c sugar
3 eggs
1 1/2 tsp vanilla extract
(optional - chocolate chips, butterscotch chips, nuts)

Preheat oven to 350 degrees. Grease a 8" x 8" baking pan. Melt butter or margarine in a large bowl. Add sugar, eggs, and vanilla extract. Mix well. In a separate bowl, mix flour, cocoa, salt, and baking powder. Add to butter mixture and mix well. (Add optional ingredients, if desired). Pour into baking pan and bake at 350 degrees for 40-45 minutes. If using a larger pan, reduce cook time.

Lemon Lush

Jeff Oren from The Rogers' Girls Family Cookbook

1 1/2 cups flour
1 1/2 cups ground walnuts
1 1/2 sticks of butter
8 oz cream cheese
1 cup powdered sugar
1 tsp vanilla
1 cup of cool whip
2 small packages instant lemon pudding
3 cups cold milk

First make the crust. Using a pastry cutter, combine flour, walnuts and butter for crust and pat into the bottom of a 9x13 pan. Bake at 325 for 30 minutes. Let cool.
Then do filling. Mix cream cheese, powdered sugar, vanilla and cool whip. Mix well and spread over cool baked crust. Refrigerate. Next make the topping. Mix packages of lemon pudding with cold milk. Once mixture has thickened, pour over filling. Top off with more cool whip and nuts if desired.

Linda's Sugar Cookies

Connie Davis from The Hixon Family Cookbook Project

1 c. butter
1-1/2 c. powdered sugar
1 egg
1 tsp. vanilla
2-1/2 c. flour

Cream butter, sugar, egg and vanilla. Add flour. Roll out on floured board. Cut with desired cutter. Bake at 350°
for 10-12 minutes. Frost/decorate as desired.

Log Cabin Cake

Mema from The Wiersch Family Cookbook

4 c. flour
1 c. cocoa
1 ½ tsp. salt
3 tsp. baking soda
3 ¾ c. sugar
1 ½ c. vegetable oil
3 c. cold coffee
3 tsp. vanilla
3 eggs

Preheat oven to 350. Sift all dry ingredients together and pour into mixer bowl. Make a well in the center of the
dry ingredients and pour all wet ingredients into the center of the well. Beat well, but batter will be runny. Pour
into a greased tube pan. Bake for one hour, or slightly longer, testing with a toothpick. Cool in pan, then flip.

Personal Notes: Original recipe called for Mazzola oil, but vegetable works fine.

Luscious Lemon Pie

Inarose Zuelke from The Zuelke Family Cookbook

1 cup sugar
6 T cornstarch
1 cup half and half
6 egg yolks, lightly beaten
1/4 cup butter
2 T lemon zest
1/2 cup lemon juice
1/2 cup sour cream
1 cup whipping cream, whipped
1 pie crust (9 inch), baked

Combine sugar and cornstarch in saucepan. Stir in half and half until smooth. Cook until thick, reduce heat and
cook two minutes more. Remove from heat. Stir a small amount of the hot mixture into the egg yolks. Return egg
yolk mixture to the pan. Cook at a gentle boil two minutes. Mixture will be VERY THICK. Remove from heat, stir
in butter and lemon zest. Gently stir in lemon juice. Cool to room temp. Fold in sour cream and whipped cream.
Pour into the pastry shell and chill before serving. Serve with additional whipped cream.

Mama's Oatmeal Cookies

Ann L. Richardson from The Richardson Family Cookbook

1 c. sugar
1 c. butter
2 eggs
1 c. sour milk
1 t. baking soda
2 1/2 c. flour
2 c. oatmeal
1 c. raisins
1/2 t. cinnamon
1/2 t. cloves
1/2 t. nutmeg
1 t. allspice
1 t. baking powder

Cream together sugar and butter. Add eggs and sour milk. Stir in baking soda, flour, oatmeal, raisins, spices and baking powder. Drop by spoonfuls onto greased cookie sheets and bake at 350° until lightly browned. Do not overbake. Let stand on cookie sheet a few minutes then remove to wire racks to cool completely.

Mashed Potato Candy

Angela Sauvageau from The Sauvageau Family Cookbook

3/4 c. mashed potatoes (cold)
4 c. powdered sugar
4 c. coconut
1/3 c. paraffin wax
12 oz. chocolate chips (or you can use 1 pkg of chocolate almond bark instead if you want)

Mix the above. I suggest adding one cup at a time of the powdered sugar and coconut to potatoes. It seems to mix better doing one cup at a time until all cups are added. Roll into walnut size balls and chill for a few hours. Melt 1 package of chocolate almond bark (or 12 oz. chocolate chips and 1/3 c. paraffin wax) and dip each ball into chocolate mixture or bark and place onto wax paper to cool/dry.

Mimi Dupree's Apricot Nectar Cake

Bonnie Davis from Our Family Cookbook

1 pkg lemon jello
1 pkg white cake mix
2/3 c. Wesson oil
2/3 c. apricot nectar
4 eggs
1 tsp. lemon juice

Preheat oven 350-375, grease tube pan. Stir together cake mix, jello, and oil. Add nectar, mix well. Add eggs one at a time and mix. Add lemon juice. Bake 45 min or until it springs back when touched. Put on topping while cake is still warm.

Lemon Glaze topping for apricot nectar cake

Take grated rind and juice of one lemon (sometimes I use bottled lemon juice, about1-2 tablespoons). Add confectioners sugar until mixture is stringy (about ½-1 cup). Pour on warm cake.

Mother McMillan's Oatmeal Cookies
Ron and Joann McMillan from McMillan Family and Friends Cookbook

1 cup margarine
1 cup brown sugar
1/2 cup sugar
1 tsp. vanilla
2 eggs
1 3/4 cup flour
1 tsp. baking soda
1 tsp. cinnamon
3 cup oatmeal
1 cup raisins
2 tbsp. grated carrots

Cream first four ingredients. Add two eggs and mix. Sift together flour, soda and cinnamon then combine with creamed ingredients. Stir in oatmeal, raisins and carrots. Drop by tablespoon on cookie sheet and bake for 10-12 minutes at 350 degrees F.

Oowey Gooey Butter Cake
Tanya Goodman from Goodman Family and Friends Cookbook Favorites

1 box yellow cake mix
1 stick butter, softened
1 egg
1 box 10x confections sugar
2 eggs
1 tsp. vanilla
1 8oz. cream cheese (softened)

Pour dry cake mix in a large bowl. Cream together with egg and softened butter. Press evenly into 13x9 glass baking dish (ungreased) forming a crust. Using a hand mixer, combine in a bowl confection sugar, eggs, vanilla and softened cream cheese. Pour on top of cake crust. Bake for 55 minutes at 350°. Let cake rest until cool, then cut.

Orange Cookies
Hilda Thompson Kilburn from A Taste of Our Family

2/3 cup shortening
3/4 cup sugar
1 egg
1/2 cup orange juice
2 tbsps. grated orange rind
2 cups all-purpose flour
1/2 tsp. baking powder
1/2 tsp. baking soda
1/2 tsp. salt
2 1/2 tbsp soft butter or margarine
1 1/2 cups sifted confectioners sugar
1 1/2 tbsp. orange juice
2 tsp. grated orange rind

Heat oven to 400° Mix shortening, 3/4 cup sugar and egg throughly. Stir in 1/2 cup orange juice and 2 tbps. rind. In another bowl measure flour by dipping & leveling method. Add baking powder, baking soda and salt to flour and mix well. Add this flour mixture to shortening mixture and blend in well.

Drop rounded tsps. of dough about 2 inches apart on ungreased baking sheet. Bake 8 to 10 mins. or until delicately browned on edges. Place on racks to cool. Frost with orange icing.

For icing, blend butter & confectioners sugar together. Stir in 1 1/2 tbsp orange juice and 2 tsp. orange rind until smooth. If icing becomes too thick add orange juice a drop or so at a time.

Personal Notes: This recipe makes a cake-like cookie.

Panattone Bread Fruit Trifle

Brenda Seals from A Double Portion

1 loaf of Pannattone bread, sliced
1 10 oz jar of lemon curd
1 8 oz packages of cream cheese
1 container of organic blueberries
1 container of organic strawberries, sliced
1 teaspoon of vanilla
½ cup of half and half

Mix cream cheese (should be room temperature) with vanilla and lemon curd, add half and half until creamy. Slice one slice of pannatone bread and tear slice up on bottom of 8 inch glass footed trifle bowl. Pour cream cheese mixture over bread. Layer with sliced strawberries. Layer with sliced torn pannatone bread. Layer with cream cheese. Layer with blueberries. Chill in refrigerator for an hour or more. Serve chilled.

Personal Notes: Use only enough half and half to get creamy consistency with cream cheese mixture.

Paula's Favorite Peppermint Cake

Paula from The Lasley's Favorite Cookbook

1 cup butter, softened
2 cups sugar
4 large eggs, separated
1/2 tsp. peppermint extract
3 cups all purpose flour
2 tsp. baking powder
1/4 tsp. salt
1 1/4 cups heavy whipping cream
1/3 cup sour cream
1/2 cup crushed peppermint candies
8 (1oz.) white chocolate squares
3/4 cup heavy whipping cream
3/4 cup butter, softened
1 tsp. vanilla extract
9 cups confectioners sugar
Garnish with peppermint sticks

Preheat oven to 350º. Spray 2 (9") round cake pans with nonstick baking spray with flour. In a large bowl, beat butter and sugar at medium speed with an electric mixer until creamy. Add egg yolks, one at a time, beating well after each addition. Beat in peppermint extract. In a medium bowl, combine flour, baking powder, and salt. Gradually add to butter mixture, alternately with cream, beginning and ending with flour mixture, beating just until combined after each addition. Stir in sour cream and crushed peppermints, just until combined. In a medium bowl, beat egg whites at high speed with an electric mixer until stiff peaks form. Gently fold into batter. Spoon batter evenly into pans. Bake for 26-28 minutes, or until a wooden pick inserted near the center comes out clean. Let cool in pans for 10 minutes. Remove from pans, and cool completely on wire racks. Wrap cake layers in heavy duty plastic wrap, and chill for at least 1 hour or up to 24 hours. For Icing: In a medium bowl, combine white chocolate and 3/4 cup cream. Microwave on high in 30 second intervals, stirring between each, until chocolate is melted and smooth about 1 1/2 minutes total. Let cool completely. In a large bowl, combine chocolate mixture and 3/4 cup butter. Beat at medium speed with an electric mixer until creamy. Add vanilla, beating until combined. Gradually add confectioners sugar, beating until smooth. Using a serrated knife, cut each layer in half horizontally to make 4 layers. Place 1 layer cut side down on a cake plate; spread with 1/2 cup frosting. Repeat procedure with remaining 3 layers. Spread tops and sides of cake with remaining frosting. Garnish with peppermint sticks, if desired.

Peatie's Perfection Light Fruit Cake

Denise Wyer from The New Donovan Family Cookbook Volume II

3/4 lb white raisins
1 1/2 cup blanched almonds, chopped
1/2 cup pecans, chopped
1 1/2 cup shredded coconut
2 lbs. candied fruit
1 cup walnut, chopped
1 cup sugar
1 cup margarine or butter
5 eggs
1 1/2 cup flour
1 tsp salt
1/2 tsp baking powder
1/4 cup pineapple juice
1 tsp vanilla
1/2 tsp almond extract

Cream sugar with shortening. Beat 5 eggs until light and gradually add to the creamed mixture. Beat well. Sift flour with salt & baking powder. Add to the batter alternately with the pineapple juice, beating well after each addition. Add vanilla and almond extract. Fold in floured fruit and nuts. Mix well. Pour into 2 loaf pans that have been lined with 2 layers of brown paper and really, really greased. Bake 275 degrees for 3 - 3 1/2 hours.

Pecan Delight Pie

Beth Medlin from Our Family Recipes

7 egg whites
2 cups sugar
1 T baking powder
1-1/2 tsp vanilla
6 oz chopped pecans
2-3/4 cup crushed soda crackers or graham crackers

Grease two 9" pie pans. Beat egg whites until stiff.
Gradually add sugar and baking powder until dissolved. Then add crackers, chopped pecans and vanilla. Divide mixture evenly. Pour into pans and bake at 325° for 30 min. When cool top with whipped topping and nuts.

Persimmon Pudding

Molly Myles Bundy from Cooking With The Cousins

4 oz. stick butter
2 c. sugar
2 eggs
2 c. persimmon pulp
1 1/2 c. buttermilk
1 tsp. soda
1 ½ c. flour
1 tsp. baking powder
½ tsp. salt
½ tsp. cinnamon
1/2 cup Milnot or Carnation canned milk
1 tsp. vanilla

Set oven to 325º. Melt butter in 9 X 13 glass pan in the oven. Beat sugar and eggs well and set aside. Mix persimmon pulp into egg mixture. Stir soda and buttermilk in 2 cup measure. In another bowl mix flour, baking powder, salt and cinnamon. Mix buttermilk and persimmon mixture. Add dry ingredients gradually, beating on low speed. Pour butter from pan into the persimmon/flour mixture and blend. Mix in milk and vanilla. Pour batter into buttered pan. Bake 55 minutes at 325º. It rises, then falls and compacts. It's done when the edges brown a little and pull away from the pan slightly. Serve warm with whipped cream or vanilla ice cream.

Personal Notes: A prize winner in the Mitchell, IN Persimmon Festival, the best persimmon pudding ever, light and almost fluffy. Instead of persimmon pulp you can use pumpkin or sweet potato.

Pineapple Crisp

Doris Parkins from Parkins Family Cookbook

1 large pineapple
1/4 c. sugar
1 T quick cooking tapioca
1 c. packed light brown sugar
1 c. all-purpose flour
1/2 c. (1 stick) cold butter, cut into small pieces

Pineapple should be peeled, quartered, cored & cut into 1 in. chunks. Heat oven to 350º. In a deep, 2 qt. baking dish, combine the pineapple, sugar & tapioca, tossing to mix well. In a medium bowl, whisk together the brown sugar & flour. Add the butter & use a pastry blender or butter knives to cut the butter into the dry ingredients until it forms a crumbly mix. Sprinkle the butter & flour mixture over the pineapple. Bake for 40 mins., or until the mixture is bubbly & the top is browned & crisp. Cool on a wire rack.

Pineapple Pie

Cathy Barbier Janet from Cathy's Favorites

Graham cracker crust - low fat
20 oz can pineapple tidbits
16 oz fat-free sour cream
1 small INSTANT vanilla pudding
1/4 cup chopped pecans (or chopped walnuts)
Cool Whip

Drain pineapple VERY well. Mix sour cream and pudding mix. Add pineapple and pecans. Place in pie crust. Chill. Top with Cool Whip

Potato Candy

Pauline Grant from Family Favorites

1 baking potato
1 c peanut butter
4 c 10x sugar

Boil potato until soft, cool, then peel and mash
Stir in 10x sugar and mix until stiff. On waxed paper, roll out mixture into 1/4 " rectangle. Spread peanut butter over entire rectangle (adjust thickness as desired). Roll up jellyroll fashion with plastic wrap and refrigerate for a few hours. Cut into slices.

Rollout Cookies

Grandma Morrell from My Grandma's Kitchen

1 c butter
1 1/2 c sugar
3 eggs
1 tsp vanilla
3 1/2 c flour
2 tsp cream of tartar
1 tsp baking soda

Preheat oven to 375. Cream butter, sugar, eggs together.
Add the rest of ingredients. Mix well. Refrigerate for 1 hour. Roll out and use desired cutter. Bake at 375 for 6 to 8 minutes.

Snicker Bar Cheese Cake

The Editor from Buzzard's Best

6- 3.7 oz Snicker bars
1 jar hot fudge sundae sauce
1 jar caramel topping
1 cup chopped roasted peanuts
1 ½ cups chocolate cookie crumbs
1 Tbl sugar
6 Tbl melted butter
10 oz bittersweet chocolate, chopped small
4 oz butter
2 eggs plus 2 yolks
1 cup sugar
1½ tsp vanilla
¾ cup flour
1 tsp baking powder
Pinch of salt
20 oz cream cheese at room temperature
2/3 cup sugar
2 eggs
1½ tsp vanilla

4 layers or steps, Crust, Fudge, Candy Bars and Cream Cheese mixture.

CRUST: Pre-heat oven to 350. Note cooling time, best to bake day before. Mix Chocolate cookie crumbs, 1 Tbl sugar, 6 Tbl melted butter together and press into bottom and 1 inch up the sides of a 10 inch spring form pan, sprayed with cooking spray. Chill.

Desserts, Pies, Cakes and Cookies

FUDGE LAYER: Melt chocolate and 4 oz butter together over very low heat stirring until just melted, set aside. With mixer, beat 2 eggs, 2 yolks, 1 cup sugar together until thick, add 1 ½ tsp vanilla, stir in chocolate mixture. Add flour, baking powder and salt. Pour into crust and bake at 350 for 20 minutes. Cool on rack while you make the cheese cake layer.

CHEESE CAKE: Mix cream cheese well, add 2/3 cup sugar and mix well, add 2 eggs one at a time mixing well, then the 1½ tsp vanilla.

Cut Snickers in ½ inch pieces and arrange all the pieces around the fudge layer evenly. They should cover most all of the fudge, BUT NOT TOUCH THE PAN SIDES.

Pour cream cheese mixture slowly and evenly over candy, Gently shake pan to even out. Bake in 350 oven 30 minutes until set, turn off oven and keep door closed for one hour. Cool and refrigerate at least 6 hours or over night.

Cut along cake and sides of pan with a thin sharp knife, remove ring from spring form. Cut in 12 pieces with long knife dipped in hot water and wiped clean after each slice. Place cake on a rack over waxed paper or cookie sheet to catch the drips. Heat hot fudge sauce in jar in microwave or in jar, in boiling water to thin syrup consistency. Dip teaspoon in hot fudge and swing back and forth in long strokes in a side ways direction, repeat until lines partially cover cheese cake in one direction. Repeat with caramel sauce in other direction making a crisscross design of both. Remove sauce dripped pan or waxed paper. Put rack over another clean sheet and pat nuts on sides of cake with cupped hands, gather nuts that fall through rack and keep adhering to side of cake. Serve with a big dollop of whipped cream.

Spicy Chocolate Jalapeño Cake

Beverly Hanson, wife of Sam Hanson from Hanson Family Cookbook

1 1/4 C. Sugar or Splenda
3/4 C. butter, softened
1 C. semi-sweet chocolate chips
1 Tsp. vanilla
3 eggs, slightly beaten
2 C. all-purpose flour
1 Tbsp. cinnamon
1 Tsp. soda
1/2 Tsp. salt
1 C. milk
1 to 2 Tbsp. finely chopped jalapeños

Melt chocolate chips and cool. Preheat oven to 350°. Beat sugar, butter and vanilla in large bowl. Add eggs; beat for 1 minute. Beat in melted chocolate chips. Combine flour, cinnamon, baking soda and salt in medium bowl; beat into mixture alternately with milk. Stir in jalapeños. Pour into well greased 9 x 13 baking pan. Bake 30 to 35 minutes or until toothpick inserted in the middle comes out clean.

Strawberry Cream Squares

Gloria Cody from All My Children Gotta Eat

2 c. graham cracker crumbs
1/3 c. butter, melted
1 (8 oz.) pkg. cream cheese
1/4 c. sugar
1 cup frozen strawberries, drained and mashed
3 c. frozen whipped topping, thawed and divided
2 boxes instant vanilla pudding
3 c. cold milk

Mix graham cracker crumbs and butter; reserve 2 tbsp. and set aside. Press remaining crumb mixture onto the bottom of a 13x9 inch pan. Combine cream cheese and sugar in a large bowl. Stir in strawberries. Fold in 2 c. whipped topping; spread evenly over crust. Beat milk and pudding mixes with whisk for 2 minutes. Pour over cream cheese mixture. Chill for 1 hour. Top with remaining whipped topping and sprinkle with reserved crumb mixture. Refrigerate at least 2 hours before serving.

Swedish Ice Cream Cake

Jacqy Lewis Soderberg from Lewis Girl's Lucky Duck Cookbook

3/4 c. all purpose flour
2 T. sugar
4 T. butter
1/2 c. firmly packed brown sugar
1/4 c. finely chopped almonds
1 T. soft butter
1 pt. coffee ice cream
1 pt. vanilla
1/2 pt. whipping cream
2 T. sugar

Butter crust chilled: Combine 3/4 c. all purpose flour with 2 T. sugar and 4 T. butter. Cut into pieces. Rub mixture with fingers until it's of even texture; pour into a 9" cake pan with removable bottom and shake to make an even layer. Press firmly on bottom and 1/2" up pan sides. Bake at 325 for 20 minutes. Chill in pan.

Praline Lace: Combine 1/2 c. firmly packed brown sugar with 1/4 c. finely chopped almonds and 1 T. soft butter. Blend evenly. On a buttered baking sheet, press mixture into an evenly thick rectangle, 6" x 8". Broil about 5" from heat until bubbling but not scorched. Let cool, then remove from pan with a wide spatula and break in large chunks. Store airtight. In chilled crust, make a layer of coffee ice cream (1 pt.), then top with vanilla (1 pt.) Whip 1/2 pt. of whipping cream until stiff with 2 T. sugar and swirl over ice cream. Freeze. Cover air tight. Remove ice cream cake from freezer 10 minutes before serving and top with praline lace. Make a border around the edge with shaved chocolate. Remove cake from pan and cut into wedges.

Toll House Pie

Stephanie Blakeman from McCarthy Family Cookbook

2 eggs
1/2 c. flour
1/2 c. white sugar
1/2 c. brown sugar
1 c. butter melted,
1 c. chocolate chips
   (cooled to room temperature)
1/4 c. chopped walnuts
9" pie crust, unbaked

Preheat oven to 325° F. In large bowl, beat eggs until foamy. Add flour, sugar, and brown sugar; beat until well blended. Blend in melted butter. Stir in chocolate chips and walnuts. Pour into pie shell. Bake at 325° F for 1 hour. Serve warm with whipped cream or ice cream.

Tropical Sour Cream Pie

Sue Chappell from The Chappell Hodge Family Cookbook

8 oz. can crushed pineapple, undrained
1 tbsp. sugar
1 c. milk
1 (4 3/4 oz.) box vanilla pudding mix
8 oz. sour cream
1 1/2 c. flaked coconut, divided
1 medium banana, sliced
4 1/2 oz. Cool Whip, thawed
1 (9 inch) pie shell, baked

Combine pineapple, sugar, milk, and pudding mix in a medium saucepan. Cook over medium heat, stirring constantly, until mixture comes to a boil. Remove from heat. Add a small amount of the hot mixture to the sour cream, mixing well. Add the rest of the sour cream to pudding mixture. Stir in 1 cup coconut. Allow to cool. Place banana slices (you may sprinkle a little lemon juice over banana slices to keep from turning brown) in pastry shell. Spoon custard mixture over bananas. Spread with whipped topping. Sprinkle remaining coconut over top. Chill at least 3 hours before serving.

Turtle Candy

Patricia Thrasher-Waller from The Thrasher Family Cookbook Project

Bag of mini pretzels
Bag of Rolo Candy
Large bag of Pecan Halves

Preheat oven to 200º. Line at least 2 cookie sheets with foil or parchment paper. Unwrap rolo candy.

Arrange pretzels on cookie sheet. Place one candy on top of each pretzel. Place in oven for 4 minutes, remove from oven and press 1 pecan halve on top of candy. Let set until firm.

White Chocolate Bread Pudding

Tiffanie Williams from Southern Family Cookbook Project

1 stick melted butter
1 tablespoon vanilla
1 cup sugar
3 beaten eggs
1 qt. half and half
1 Loaf of brown sugar cinnamon bread
1/2 stick melted butter
6 oz. white chocolate
1/2 tsp. vanilla
1/2 cup powdered sugar

To make pudding, break bread into pieces and place in 10 x 13 glass dish. Mix 1 tablespoon vanilla, 1 cup sugar, eggs, and half and half, melted butter, then pour over bread. Bake at 350 for 50 minutes.

To make sauce, melt 1/2 stick butter in microwave, then add white chocolate. Stir and heat again until melted. stir in powdered sugar and 1/2 tsp. vanillla. Pour over pudding while hot. If this is too thick, add a little whole milk.

Lemon Curd for "Afternoon Tea" pg. 167

Miscellaneous

Stuffed Strawberries pg. 170

White Chocolate Macadamia Nut Bark pg. 170

3 layer Jello Mold

Susan Privot from Family Recipes

3 large boxes of jello - 2 green and 1 red for Christmas
 or 1 pink, one yellow, one orange for Easter
8 oz cool whip
8 oz vanilla yogurt for each box of jello
Key lime or lemon yogurt

To each box of jello, add 1 1/2 c boiling water. When dissolved, stir in 2 c ice cubes until gelatin is thickened. Remove ice chips, blend with 8 oz yogurt. Put in bottom of trifle dish to set.

Repeat with the other 2 colors of jello, alternating with Cool whip or Yogurt as the additive.

Yum.

Aunt Alma's Pickles - Sweet Garlic Dills
Heather Daniel-Blake from Joy of the Repast: Favorite Recipes of Family and Friends

4 c. sugar
1/2 c. canning salt
1 qt. white vinegar
2 c. water
small cucumbers, unpeeled
dill - fresh weed or seed
garlic cloves, optional
hot peppers, optional

Wash and slice the cucumbers. To make the brine, bring sugar, salt, vinegar, and water to a boil until salt and sugar are dissolved.
Pack the cucumbers into pint jars, alternately with dill, garlic and peppers, if desired. Pour boiling vinegar mixture over cucumbers. Screw on hot lids. If jars do not seal, store them in refrigerator. Wait two weeks before eating.

Personal Notes: Garlic and peppers can be sliced and boiled with the brine and then discarded before pouring brine into jars.

Breakfast Pizza

Tanya Goodman from Goodman Family and Friends Cookbook Favorites

1 pizza shell
8 eggs
1 pd. lean ground beef or sausage
green pepper
onion
salt and pepper to taste

Preheat oven to 400°. Brown ground beef or sausage and drain. Scramble eggs. Saute or steam cut up vegetables, al dente. Take pizza shell and add scrambled eggs to cover shell. Layer meat, green pepper and onion. Top with cheese and sprinkle with salt and pepper. Cook in oven for about 15 minutes or until cheese is melted and crust is lightly brown.

Cereal Bars

Linda Farinella from The Anderson / Farinella Family Cookbook

4 cups Rice Krispies
4 cups Cheerios
2 cups dry roasted nuts
1 cup mini M&Ms (optional)
1cup light corn syrup
1 cup white sugar
1 cup creamy peanut butter
1 tsp vanilla

Toss in large bowl all dry ingredients. Lightly grease a 10x15 pizza pan. In a sauce pan over medium heat stir together corn syrup, sugar and peanut butter. Bring mixture to a boil and cook until sugar is dissolved. Remove from heat and add peanut butter and vanilla. Pour the mixture into the bowl and mix well. Press into pan. Let cool. Cut into squares or bars.

Cheese Fondue (with Wine) From Deb

Mama from Mama's Little Black Book and More

1 clove garlic, halved
1-1/2 cups dry white wine
1 lb. cheese, grated
2 tsp. cornstarch or arrowroot
3 tbsp. Kirsch
fresh pepper
crusty bread--2-3 baguettes

Cut bread into bite-sized cubes and set aside. Rub a fondue pot, or something which can be put over a flame, or an electric fondue pot, with garlic, then add wine. Blend the cornstarch with the Kirsch and set aside.

Heat the wine almost to boiling, but don't boil. Add cheese VERY slowly, one handful at a time, while stirring with a wooden spoon. If the cheese begins to separate from the liquid, try reducing heat. When the cheese is creamy and barely simmering, add cornstarch mixture to pot. Stir until mixture bubbles, and add pepper to taste. Keep warm at the table over a low flame (or keep the electric pot plugged in), and serve immediately with cubes of bread and long fondue forks.

Personal Notes: For cheese use half Emmenthaler, half Gruyere.

Cheesy Chicken Dip

Stephanie Sackett from Edie's Family Cookbook

4 c. cooked, chopped chicken
3/4 onion, chopped
1 lb. velveeta, cubed
1 8oz. pkg. cream cheese, cubed
10.5oz. can cream of chicken soup
1 c. mayonnaise
1/2 c. medium salsa
1/2 tsp. garlic powder

Dump all ingredients together in crock pot or oven safe dish. For crock pot cook on low for 2-3 hours or high for 1 hour. For oven bake at 350º for about 30 minutes. Stir occasionally while baking or in crock pot. Serve with tortilla chips.

Coconut Crescents

Ann L. Richardson from The Richardson Family Cookbook

2 T. butter
2 T. water
1 t. vanilla extract
2 c. confectioner's sugar
1/2 c. instant nonfat dry milk
2 2/3 c. flaked coconut
4 squares semi-sweet chocolate
1 T. shortening

Melt butter in saucepan. Add water and vanilla. Combine confectioner's sugar and dry milk. Stir into butter mixture 1/2 cup at a time mixing well after each addition. Blend in coconut. For each candy, shape about 1 T. mixture into a roll 2" long; curve into a crescent. Refrigerate until firm, about 15 minutes. Melt chocolate and shortening over hot water. Remove from heat and let stand to cool slightly. Dip each piece of candy halfway into chocolate. Place on waxed paper to dry. Refrigerate until firm. Store in air-tight container.

Crazy Crust Pizza

Eva Taft Snyder from The Snyder/Johnson Family Cookbook Project

1 cup flour
1 tsp. salt
1 tsp. oregano
1/8 tsp. pepper
2 eggs
2/3 cup milk

Mix ingredients. Pour on well-greased pans. Put your pepperoni, mushrooms, etc on top; bake at 425º, for 25 minutes. Take out of oven and put tomato sauce on cheese on top. Bake an additional 10 minutes.

Flat Bread Pizza

Geri Rusch from My Grandma's Kitchen

5 c Flour
1 tsp Baking Soda
1 tsp White Pepper
1 tsp Sugar
2 tsp Salt
1 c Buttermilk
1 c Water
Olive Oil Cooking Spray
Roma Tomatoes, sliced
Fresh Basil, finely chopped
Campazola Cheese, cut into cubes

Mix together everything except Tomatoes, Basil and Campazola Cheese in a large bowl. Knead until smooth. Divide portion in half. Roll out ½ the bread dough into a rectangle shape. Spray with Olive Oil.
Preheat grill on high. When grill is hot turn to low.
Put dough, olive oil side down on the grill and cook for a few minutes until he bottom is no longer doughy. Spray the top side with olive oil and flip it over to cook the top side. When the top side is firm add the toppings. Cook until cheese is melted. Repeat process for other half of bread dough. Cut and serve.

Personal Notes: Note you can use any toppings you want

Miscellaneous

Four-Grain Flapjacks

Tara Vieth from Cookin' with Balls II

1cup whole-wheat flour
3/4 cup all-purpose flour
1/3 cup stone ground cornmeal
1/4 cup rolled oats
2 tablespoons sugar
2 teaspoons baking powder
1 teaspoon salt
1/2 teaspoon baking soda
1/2 teaspoon ground cinnamon
Pinch of freshly ground nutmeg
 1 3/4 cups milk
1/4 cup honey
3 large eggs
4 tablespoons (1/2 stick) unsalted butter, melted

Prepare and preheat your griddle. Whisk together dry ingredients in a large bowl. Whisk together wet ingredients in another bowl. Pour the wet ingredients over the dry ingredients and gently whisk them together, mixing just until combined. Spoon 1/4 cup batter onto the griddle for each pancake, nudging the batter into rounds. Cook until the top of each pancake is speckled with bubbles and some bubbles have popped, then turn and cook until the underside is lightly browned. Serve immediately or keep warm in a 200 degree oven while you finish cooking the rest.

Personal Notes: We add blueberries and they are delicious!

Goat Cheese, Artichoke and Smoked Ham Strata

Michelle Rice from The New Donovan Family Cookbook Volume II

2 c. whole milk
1/4 c. olive oil
8 c. sourdough bread
1 1/2 c. whipping cream
5 large eggs
1 T. chopped garlic
1 1/2 tsp salt
3/4 tsp black pepper
1/2 tsp ground nutmeg
12 oz. soft fresh goat cheese
2 T chopped fresh sage
1 T chopped fresh thyme
1 1/2 tsp herbes de Provence
12 oz smoked ham, chopped
2 1/2 cups marinated artichoke hearts
1 c. grated Fontina cheese
1 1/2 c. grated Parmesan

Crumble goat cheese. drain and chop marinated artichoke hearts. Trim crusts and cut bread into 1- inch cubes. Preheat oven to 350 degrees. Butter 13 x 9 glass baking dish. Whisk milk and oil in large bowl. Stir in bread. Let stand until liquid is absorbed, about 10 minutes. In blender mix together next set of ingredients. In a bowl mix together the Fontina and Parmesan cheeses.

Place half of bread mixture in prepared dish. Top with half of ham, artichoke hearts, and cheeses. Pour half of cream egg mixture over. Repeat layering. Can be made 1 day ahead. Cover, chill.

Bake uncovered until firm in center and brown around edges, about 1 hour.

Grandma Kenville's Turkey Stuffing

Kimberly Story from The Cookbook of Our Favorite Foods and Memories

Giblets
1 med onion, diced
1 sm stock of celery, diced
Salt and pepper to taste
1 c raisins
2 apples, cored
3 packets Stove Top Stuffing Mix

Put giblets, 1/2 of the onion, celery, salt and pepper in a pan. Cover with water and cook until giblets are tender. Put in the fridge over night. The next day, make the Stove Top Stuffing according to the directions. Remove the giblets for the stock, keeping the stock for future use. Grind giblets, raisins, apples and the rest of the onion. Add mixture (about 4 cups) and stock to the stuffing and stir. Put stuffing in a casserole dish, cover and bake at 350° for 50 minutes. Remove the cover and bake for another 10 minutes.

Korean BBQ Skewers

Diane Paul from The Wedding Cookbook for Jenna and Adam

2 lb boneless sirloin steaks
1/3 cup brown sugar
3 tbsp. honey
1/4 cup toasted sesame oil
1/2 cup soy sauce
4 scallions, sliced into thin rings
3 garlic cloves, finely chopped
1/2 cup toasted sesame seeds
2 tbsp. flour
1/2 cup water

Soak wooden skewers in water to prevent burning. Can soak while you prepare the meat. Cut meat into thin strips about 1 1/2 inches long for skewers. Toast sesame seeds in saute pan, stirring often to keep from burning. They should be a nice golden brown. Mix all the ingredients, including the sesame seeds, then add the beef and refrigerate for one or more hours or even overnight. Thread the beef onto skewers. Grill or place under broiler until desired doneness. Turn once.

Lemon Curd for "Afternoon Tea"

Anne Stokes from A. T. Cooks   "Afternoon Tea"   and other family recipes

4 large eggs
1 c. sugar
1 t. grated lemon peel
1/2 c. lemon juice
1/2 c. (1/4) lb. butter, cut into chunks
Baked Tartlet Shells

In the top of a double boiler combine eggs, sugar, lemon peel and lemon juice, mix well, add butter. Stir over simmering water until lemon curd is thick enough to mound slightly; approx. 10 min. Remove from heat and let cool, then cover and chill until cold. Stir and spoon equally into tart shells.

Mexi-Stack

The Editor from Buzzard's Best

2 corn tortillas
1 ¼ inch thick slice of ham
½ cup grated Jack Cheese
2 eggs
½ Tomatillo or Ranchero sauce

Heat a griddle to high, add some oil and wipe with paper towel. Place 2 tortillas on hot griddle, and ham next to it. Cook tortilla about 30 seconds and turn over. Sprinkle half of the cheese on each of the tortillas, and place the heated ham on the cheese on one of the tortillas. Carefully turn one tortilla on to the other sandwich style, press lightly with spatula to flatten . Turn and cook a little longer until cheese is almost melted.

Place on a oven proof plate or cookie sheet. Heat sauce to simmer and turn off. Top Tortilla sandwich with 2 over easy (or cooked to your liking) eggs. Do not add sauce until all eggs are cooked and on tortillas. Spoon heated sauce on eggs, sprinkle with cheese and bake until cheese is melted. Garnish with Sour cream, Salsa fresca, Avocado slices, Cilantro and/or Pickled jalapeno peppers. Serve with Re-fried or black beans.

Orange Spiced Nuts

Suzanne Dunscomb from Bennett's & Beyond: A Family Cookbook

3 cups nuts
1 cup sugar
1/3 cup orange juice
1 Tbsp. cinnamon
1/2 tsp. salt
1/2 tsp. ground cloves

Heat oven to 275°F. Spread nuts on ungreased 15x10-inch cookie sheet. Bake at 275°F. for 10 minutes. In medium saucepan, combine sugar, orange juice, cinnamon, salt and ground cloves. Bring to a boil; boil 2 minutes, stirring occasionally. Remove from heat; stir in nuts. Using a slotted spoon, remove nuts to waxed paper. Separate with fork; let dry. Store in airtight container in cool dry place.

Personal Notes: You can use pecans, peanuts, mixed nuts, walnuts, etc. Any nuts will due, it is a matter of personal preference.

Party Pretzel Mix

Maria de la Calle from The Wiersch Family Cookbook

1 16 oz. package large pretzels
3/4 cup vegetable oil
1/2 tsp. garlic powder
1/2 tsp. dill (dried)
2 2-oz. packages dry Ranch salad dressing mix

Preheat oven to 200*. Break pretzels into bite-sized pieces. Place in large mixing bowl. In a small separate bowl, combine all remaining ingredients and whisk well. Pour over pretzels; toss to coat. Place onto ungreased baking sheet. Place in oven for 1 hour, stirring approx. every 15 minutes.

Peanut Butter and Jelly French Toast

Marilee Larkey from Mom Loves to Cook

12 slices of bread
3/4 cup peanut butter
6 T. jelly or jam
3 eggs
3/4 cup milk
1/4 t. salt
2 T. butter or margarine

Spread peanut butter on six slices of bread; spread jelly on other six slices of bread. Put one slice of each together to form sandwiches. In mixing bowl, lightly beat eggs; add milk and salt and mix together. Melt butter in a large skillet over medium heat. Dip sandwiches in egg mixture, coating well. Place in skillet and brown both sides. Serve immediately.

Polly's Sausage Quiche

Milly Noah from Grits to Gourmet

2 9" shallow pie crusts
1 lb. hot sausage, cooked and drained
4 eggs, beaten
2/3 cup whole milk
1 cup sharp cheddar cheese, grated
1 cup Swiss cheese, grated
1 8oz. carton regular sour cream
1 tsp. dry mustard

Divide cooked sausage between pie shells. Divide the two cheeses between the two shells. Mix eggs, milk, mustard, and sour cream. Pour mixture over the two pies. Bake 1 hour in a preheated 350 degree oven on bottom shelf.

Pumpkin Pie Dip

Shanna Lasley from The Lasley's Favorite Cookbook

1 pkg. cream cheese, softened
2 cups confectioners sugar
1 cup canned pumpkin
1/2 cup sour cream
1 tsp. ground cinnamon
1 tsp. pumpkin pie spice
1/2 tsp. ground ginger
Gingersnap Cookies

In large mixing bowl, beat cream cheese and sugar until smooth. Beat in the pumpkin, sour cream and spices until blended. Serve with gingersnaps.

Miscellaneous

Snow Ice Cream

The Editor from Mom's Favorite Recipes

5 eggs
2 c. milk
1 c. sugar
1 t. vanilla
 a little salt

After a big snowfall, take a large pan or bowl outside and fill it with CLEAN (no yellow allowed) snow. Leave it outside while you mix the above ingredients until smooth. Bring in the snow and add it to the mixture until it turns into ice cream.

Stuffed Strawberries

Jackie Shields from The Jones-Simpson Cookbook

1 pint strawberries, washed
8 oz. softened cream cheese
Powdered sugar to taste
1-2 tsp. Grand Marnier (optional)

Cut stems off berries. Cut a crisscross slice 3/4 of the way down the opposite (pointed) end of each berry. Beat cream cheese, a small amount powdered sugar and Grand Marnier until smooth. Do not use too much powdered sugar or liquer as mixture will be too thin. Place in a pastry bag with a star tip. Pipe mixture into the center of each cut berry. Refrigerate until serving.

Very Veggie Pizza Squares

The Editor from Home Sweet Home Recipes

2 packages Crescent rolls
3/4 cup mayonnaise
2 8 oz packages cream cheese
1 package dry ranch dressing mix
1 c. chopped broccoli
1 c. chopped cauliflower
1 c. chopped carrots
2 c. shredded mild cheddar cheese

Preheat oven to 350°. Spray cookie sheet with Pam.
Spread Crescent rolls on cookie sheet and pinch seams together. Bake 8 to10 minutes. Cool.

Combine mayonnaise, softened cream cheese and ranch dressing mix. Spread over cooled crust. Top with chopped vegetables. Sprinkle with shredded cheese. Cut into squares.

White Chocolate Macadamia Nut Bark

Anneta Sudlow - Cooper Tire & Rubber Company from The Toledo Area Chapter APA Celebrates National Payroll Week!

2 cups semisweet chocolate morsels
2 cups white morsels
2/3 cup toasted macadamia nuts or toasted almonds, coarsely chopped

Line a 13 by 9-inch cookie sheet with waxed paper, allowing 2 inches of paper to hang over sides. Melt all but 1/4

cup of semisweet chocolate morsels in microwave on medium power for 2 minutes, stirring every 30 seconds, or until smooth. Pour chocolate onto prepared sheet and spread to cover entire surface and form 1 even layer. Melt all but 1/4 cup of white chips in microwave on medium power for 2 minutes, stirring every 30 seconds, or until smooth. Drizzle melted white chocolate over semisweet chocolate layer. Using a toothpick or skewer, swirl the melted chocolates together, creating a marbled effect.
Place nuts in a plastic bag and crush, using a rolling pin. Sprinkle chocolate with nuts and remaining semisweet and white morsels. Gently press toppings into melted chocolates. Refrigerate for 30 minutes, or until chocolate is firm. Remove waxed paper from chocolate. Cut or break chocolate into bite-size pieces.

Personal Notes: For chocolate I recommend Guittard Choc-Au-Lait.

Ziploc Omelet

Mi Mi Spak and Delaney Upton from McKee Cooks

quart-size Ziploc freezer bag
2 lg. or extra lg. eggs
cheese
onions
green pepper
bacon bits
ham,
hash browns

Write names on Ziploc bags with magic marker. Put eggs into the bag (no more than 2). Shake and combine. Add cheese, meat, vegetables as desired. Remove all air from bag and zip it up (make sure bag is closed tight). Place bag in rolling boiling water for exactly 13 minutes. Open bag and omelet will roll out.

Notes

Notes

Index of Recipes

Index of Recipes by Category

Index of Recipes by Contributor

Best of the Family Cookbook Project Cookbook

Need additional copies of this cookbook to share with friends and family, go to www.BestCookbookProject.com and order your copies today.

Best of the Family Cookbook Project Cookbook is also available from Amazon.com and many fine local bookstores.

Start Your Own Family Cookbook

Tired of collecting recipes in an overflowing box or notebook? Want recipes from other members of your family? Want recipes online as well as in a beautiful cookbook such as this one? Don't know where to start?

FamilyCookbookProject.com will make it easy for you!

Our easy-to –use, step by step website will help you create and print a beautiful personalized cookbook that will be cherished forever. Whether it is a personal cookbook with only your recipes or you invite the entire extended family to contribute, you will be impressed with the results.

Creating your own personalized family cookbook is as easy as creating an account, inviting others to contribute using our automatic email invitation program, entering your own recipes, selecting options such as cover, welcome message and cookbook name and sending the cookbook to print – it's that easy.

Get started today at www.FamilyCookbookProject.com